The Flute Book

Melvin Berger

THE FLUTE BOOK

ILLUSTRATED WITH PHOTOGRAPHS

Lothrop, Lee & Shepard Co. ❧ *New York*

Also by Melvin Berger
THE VIOLIN BOOK
MASTERS OF MODERN MUSIC

Library of Congress Cataloging in Publication Data

Berger, Melvin.
　The flute book.

　Discography: p.
　1. Flute—Juvenile literature.　I. Title.
ML3930.A2B495　　788'.51　　72-12873
ISBN 0-688-41296-3
ISBN 0-688-51296-8 (lib. bdg.)

COPYRIGHT © 1973 BY MELVIN BERGER

All rights reserved. No part of this book may be reproduced or utilized in any form or by any means, electronic or mechanical, including photocopying, recording or by any information storage and retrieval system, without permission in writing from the Publisher. Inquiries should be addressed to Lothrop, Lee and Shepard Company, 105 Madison Ave., New York, N. Y. 10016.

PRINTED IN THE UNITED STATES OF AMERICA.

1　2　3　4　5　77　76　75　74　73

Acknowledgments

I wish to acknowledge the generous help given me in the writing of this book by flute players Ruth Freeman and Samuel Baron, and by flute makers Lewis J. Deveau of Wm. Haynes and Mark Thomas of W. T. Armstrong. In addition, my thanks go to my fellow musicians in the American Symphony and Chautauqua Symphony for sharing their thoughts and ideas with me, and to the staff of the Library and Museum of the Performing Arts in Lincoln Center for assisting me in the use of their unique research facilities.

FOR ELEANOR—*the fairest flutist of them all.*

Contents

1 YOU AND THE FLUTE 11

2 OF FLUTES AND PICCOLOS 32

3 SCIENCE AND THE FLUTE 54

4 HISTORY OF THE FLUTE 62

5 FLUTE MAKERS 85

6 FLUTE PLAYERS 99

GLOSSARY 117

THE FLUTE ON RECORDS 120

INDEX 123

The flute is one of the most popular of all musical instruments.
Photograph by Melvin Berger

CHAPTER ONE

You and the Flute

The flute is one of the oldest and most popular of all musical instruments. All over the world, and at all times, people have played the flute.

Today's flutes have a beautiful, clear, ringing sound. No wonder about 1 million boys and girls, and men and women play the flute. And every year about 100,000 young people start to study the flute. Countless millions more listen to flute players at concerts, at musical shows, in opera and ballet performances, and in the bands at parades and football games. Perhaps you, too, like the sound of the flute. Perhaps you play, or have thought of playing, the flute.

FLUTE LESSONS

You need three things to be able to play the flute: a desire to play, a teacher, and an instrument.

Learning to play *any* instrument involves talent, finger dex-

Flute teacher Robert Keating plays along with his class.
Photograph by Melvin Berger

terity, and a good ear. But the desire to play is most important. If you really want to play, and you have no serious breathing problem and your teeth and lips are normal, you can become a flutist.

Some people call flute players flautists. This comes from *flauto*, the Italian word for flute. If you choose to be a flutist, or flautist (both names are correct), you need a teacher. He teaches you the skills of playing, just as he learned them from his teacher. He passes on to you a tradition of flute playing that goes back many centuries. That is how the great heritage of flute playing is kept alive and carried into the future.

Your first flute lessons may take place in school, where the music teacher gives lessons to groups of children. Usually you do not have to pay for lessons in school. Or, you may learn to play the flute outside of school, where the teacher works with one student at a time. These are called private lessons. Private lessons are given in your home, in the teacher's home, or at a music school. Usually you pay for private lessons.

New flutes range in cost from about two-hundred to one-thousand dollars and more; used flutes cost less, of course. To start, you want one that is not very expensive, yet that is easy to play and sounds good. In choosing a flute, new or used, you must be sure that no air leaks out through the pads that cover the holes of the flute. Ask your teacher or the salesman to check the pads before you buy or rent a flute.

The beginning flute student usually takes one lesson a week. At the first lesson you usually learn about the three parts of the flute. It has a top piece, or head joint, with a mouth hole; a main piece, or body joint, with tone holes, keys and pads to cover the holes, and rods to hold the keys; and an end piece, or foot joint, also with holes, keys, pads, and rods.

Your teacher shows you how to put the three parts together without damaging the delicate mechanism of the flute. Hold

Grasp the parts very carefully when you assemble the flute.
Photograph by Melvin Berger

Ruth Freeman, an outstanding flutist and teacher, demonstrates for her student at a private lesson.   *Photograph by Melvin Berger*

the head joint with one hand, and grasp the body joint with the other hand above the keys and rods. Be careful not to press on the rods with your hand, as they might bend out of shape and the flute will not play.

Gently twist the head joint as you slip it into the body. Do not force it, and do not rock it back and forth. If the ends are clean, they should fit together tightly without being forced. Never use oil or grease on the ends. Join the foot joint to the body in the same careful way, holding the body joint above the keys and the foot joint below the keys.

The mouth hole in the head joint should line up with the first key on the body joint. The middle of the last key on the body should line up with the rod on the foot joint. After a few tries, you will find it very easy to put the flute together as well as to take it apart.

Once your flute is together, you will start to play. Your teacher will show you how to hold the flute with the lip plate

Once the parts of the flute are assembled, it is a good idea to make sure they are lined up correctly.   *Photograph by Melvin Berger*

resting beneath your lower lip, and the end of the flute pointing down at about a 20-degree angle. Your arms are held away from your body, with your thumbs under the flute and your fingertips covering the keys.

Your teacher will explain how to form your lips and mouth. This is called the "embouchure." The correct embouchure directs just the right amount of air in the right direction across the mouth hole. A good embouchure is very important in producing a beautiful tone on the flute.

To play a note you touch the tip of your tongue to the gum above your upper teeth as though you were going to say "too." Pull back your tongue and release the air. This is called tonguing. Tonguing gives each note a sharp, clean beginning. Tonguing is used to start notes; it is never used to end notes.

Once you start flute lessons, you become very aware of how you breathe. When you inhale, your diaphragm moves down and your ribs move up and out. (The diaphragm is the large sheet of muscles that separates the chest from the abdomen.) Air rushes into your lungs through your nose and mouth. When you exhale you force the air out again.

A flute player needs to inhale a lot of air quickly, and then exhale the air very slowly. Your teacher will show you how to use your diaphragm, ribs, and embouchure to control your breathing.

When you know how to hold the flute and how to produce a sound, you are ready to learn how to read music. Your teacher will probably choose a method book for you. The method book will develop your skill in reading music and in playing the flute.

The most famous embouchure in the world: a close-up of Jean-Pierre Rampal. *Photograph courtesy Colbert Artists Management*

At each lesson the teacher will go over the exercises in the book. He will teach you how to read the notes and how to play them. He will remind you over and over again about the right way to hold the flute, the correct embouchure, and how to control the way you breathe. He will help you make a little air go a long way. Before too long you will be getting beautiful sounds from the flute—without the dizziness that often bothers beginners on the instrument.

You will be learning something new all the time: new notes, new rhythms, and new techniques. During the week you will practice at home what you have learned at your lesson, going over the difficult parts until you can do them easily and well. The speed of your progress will depend on how well you practice at home.

As you go along, you will go on to more and more interesting music. You will also learn more advanced ways of playing the flute.

You will learn double tonguing. Double tonguing is used for playing very fast notes when it is difficult or impossible to say "too-too-too" fast enough. In double tonguing you say "too-koo-too-koo." (Some teachers prefer tee-hee or doo-goo.) See how fast you can repeat the "toos." Then try the "too-koos." You will find that the "too-koos" of double tonguing go much, much faster. Double tonguing allows you to play very rapid separate notes.

Good flute players also learn to play with vibrato. Vibrato is a smooth, even tremble of the flute tone that makes it sound more like a beautiful human voice. You develop a flute vibrato by learning how to produce a rapid shaking in your diaphragm and throat.

Flutter tonguing is a special effect used on the flute. It gives the tone a strange-sounding wobble. To do flutter tonguing the flutist rolls the letter r-r-r-r-r with his tongue as he plays.

It takes time and hard work to master the flute. But any flutist will tell you that it certainly is worth the effort.

CARING FOR THE FLUTE

Each time you play the flute, moisture from your breath collects in the tube of the instrument. Before you put it away in its case, you should dry the inside of the flute. Use the cleaning rod that comes with it. Thread a clean, soft cloth through the hole in the rod. An old handkerchief is fine.

Take the flute apart and push the rod and cloth back and forth into each section. Return each piece to the case as soon as it is clean. If you clean and dry your flute before you put it away, it will be free of dirt and germs. It will also prevent damage to the pads, and the flute will play more easily.

The student keeps her flute clean by pushing the rod and an old handkerchief through the tube. *Photograph by Melvin Berger*

To keep the flute bright and shiny on the outside wipe it with a soft, clean cloth. Never use silver polish or any other cleaner. Polishes can make the keys stick and quickly spoil the pads.

Keep the flute in its case when you are not playing on it. The case keeps out the dust that can jam the action. It also prevents damage from accidents like bumps or scratches.

Make sure the case is kept away from heaters or windows or closed cars. Any place that gets very hot or very cold is not a good place for your flute. Last, but not least, remember to keep it away from curious brothers and sisters. A shiny flute may look like a wonderful toy to a young child.

PLAYING IN SCHOOL

Most schools allow students to study the flute when they are in the fourth or fifth grade. In a short while these flutists go into the school band or orchestra. The band has many flutists; the orchestra has just a few. Some players prefer the band, some prefer the orchestra, and some choose to play in both.

In elementary school bands and orchestras, you usually perform music that was composed for school use. These pieces are fun to play and help you to master your instrument. Sometimes these groups play simple arrangements of well-known pieces of music.

In junior and senior high schools, you begin to play great pieces of music, just as they were written by world-famous composers. Part of the time the flute plays the melody, either accompanied by other instruments in the groups, or all alone.

Wiping the outside of the flute with a soft clean cloth keeps it looking shiny. *Photograph by Melvin Berger*

Several flutists play in the elementary school band.
Photograph by Melvin Berger

Other times the flute plays a background accompaniment when other instruments are playing the melody. Quite often the flute plays together with the other members of the woodwind family of instruments, the oboe, clarinet, and bassoon.

Bands and orchestras in school usually play at assemblies and concerts. But the players sometimes perform in other groups as well. There is the marching band, for example, that plays in parades and at football games. Most players wear uniforms when they perform in a marching band.

Flutists in a high school band often wear uniforms at concerts.
Photograph by Melvin Berger

A good number of schools have a band that just plays pop music. It may be called a jazz band, dance band, or stage band. In these bands, the flute is used mostly for solos and special effects.

In some schools there are musical groups for flutists who

Two flutists play piccolos in this marching band rehearsal.
Photograph by Melvin Berger

One of the numbers played by the high school jazz band features a flute solo. *Photograph by Melvin Berger*

want to play with a few other players. Music for these groups, with only one person playing each part, is called chamber music.

Two popular chamber-music combinations are the woodwind quintet—flute, oboe, clarinet, bassoon, and French horn—and the woodwind quartet, which is the same, but without the French horn. There is also chamber music for flute and string instruments. The flute quartet—flute, violin, viola, and cello—and the flute trio, which is the same but without a cello, are the popular flute and string groups.

While you are studying the flute, you may have a few chances to play solos at concerts or recitals. There are many excellent solo works for the flute that you can choose from.

Student flutists as well as concert artists often perform sonatas. A flute sonata is usually a piece for flute with piano accompaniment. Most sonatas take about fifteen minutes to play. They are divided into separate sections called movements.

The concerto is another form of flute music. When a flutist plays a concerto, he or she stands in front of the accompanying orchestra. In student performances the orchestra part may be played on a piano. Concertos usually have just three movements.

In addition to the sonatas and concertos, there are any number of incidental solo works for the flute. There are waltzes, marches, caprices, minuets, variations, scherzos, and many, many other types and forms of music. In fact, the list seems to go on without end, because composers are always writing new solos for the flute.

FLUTE PLAYING AS A PROFESSION

After studying and playing for many years, some flutists find that they enjoy the flute very, very much. In fact, they enjoy it more than anything else they do. They play very well and have had success playing in school groups and as soloists. They want to make playing the flute their life's work—their profession.

Some professional flutists become teachers. They give private flute lessons to children and grown-ups. They may take special college courses that prepare them to teach the flute to children in schools, colleges, or music conservatories. School music teachers usually are able to play several instruments and can conduct an orchestra or band.

Many highly trained flutists work in the 120 professional symphony orchestras in the United States. Each of the full-

The four flutists stand at the microphone when they play a solo with the United States Army Field Band.
*Photograph by William R. Bope, courtesy of
U. S. Army Field Band*

sized orchestras has four flute players. Some smaller groups have only two or three flutists. These professional orchestras rehearse about three hours a day and give two or more concerts a week. Flutists in an orchestra sit near the center of the stage, just behind the violinists.

There are professional flutists in the orchestras at radio or television stations and recording companies. There are flutists

Flutists in the orchestra are seated near the other woodwind instruments—the oboes, clarinets, and bassoons.
*Photograph by Bert Bial, courtesy
N.Y. Philharmonic*

at every opera, ballet, or musical show that uses an orchestra. These orchestras are often hidden beneath the front of the stage in the orchestra pit. Look for them the next time you are in a theater.

There are flutists who play only in chamber-music groups and those who play pop music in small groups. Almost all performing groups include a flute player.

Do you see the two flutists in the orchestra on stage at Philharmonic Hall in New York's Lincoln Center?

Photograph by Sandor Acs, courtesy N.Y. Philharmonic

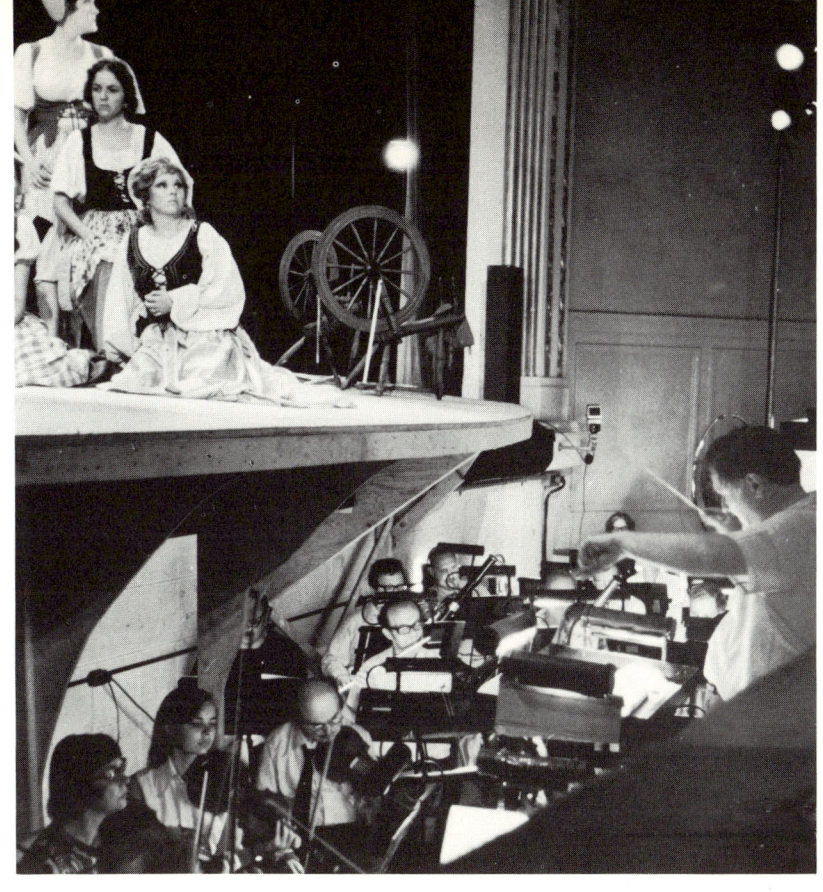
The musicians are crowded in the pit during an opera rehearsal.
Photograph by Melvin Berger

At the very top of the profession are the few flutists who become soloists. These soloists are born with a great talent for playing the flute. In addition, they have always spent many hours every day practicing the flute. They are masters of flute playing.

Flute soloists give recitals where they are accompanied by the piano. They perform concertos with orchestras. They thrill audiences everywhere with rapid passages, warm, beautiful tones, and haunting melodies.

Many flutists learn to play the flute and enjoy playing but do not want to make it their life work. They want to continue

Karl Kraber is the flutist in the well-known Dorian Woodwind Quintet. The other players are Charles Kuskin, oboe; Barry Benjamin, French horn; June Taylor, bassoon; and Jerry Kirkbride, clarinet.
Photograph courtesy Columbia Artists Management Inc.

with the flute as a hobby. These players usually find places in one of the 1,400 amateur orchestras in America. Or they perform with one of the amateur bands that are found in many cities.

Amateur orchestras and bands usually rehearse in the evening. Students, doctors, homemakers, teachers, and businessmen who are busy all day take part. These groups usually give a few concerts during the year.

Most flutists, professional or amateur, are very excited about their chosen instrument. In some cities they have formed flute clubs. The flute clubs arrange concerts, have lectures and demonstrations on the flute, play for each other, and in general, try to learn more about the instrument. See if there is an active flute club near where you live. Try to attend some meetings. If there is no club nearby, perhaps you can help to start one in your community.

This amateur flutist enjoys playing in the park on summer Sunday afternoons. *Photograph by Melvin Berger*

CHAPTER TWO

Of Flutes and Piccolos

The flute is a delicate and precise work of craftsmanship. Flute-makers must be very skillful and precise as they create a musical instrument from a hollow tube of metal.

Each part of the flute—tube, holes, pads, keys, and rods—must be perfect by itself. Each part must be exactly the right size and shape, and must be placed in exactly the right spot. But, more than that, all the parts must work perfectly together and last through years and years of playing.

Most professionals and advanced students play on flutes that are made of silver. The silver is either coin silver, which is almost pure silver with just a small percentage of copper added to make the silver harder and stronger; or sterling silver, which is also nearly pure silver. A few performers play on very expensive gold flutes. Even rarer are the players who own and use platinum flutes.

Students' flutes are usually made of a metal called nickel silver. Nickel silver does not contain any silver at all. Instead it is an alloy of three metals: copper, zinc, and nickel The exact amount of each metal is a closely guarded secret of the different flute makers. Usually it is about 62 percent copper, 20 percent zinc, and 18 percent nickel.

One maker, working alone, would need about three-and-one-half weeks to build a flute. So most flutes are made by more than one person. They are built in flute factories, where the work is divided among several craftsmen. Each worker is responsible for just a small part of the entire operation, from the first steps to the finished flute.

It is usually very quiet in the factory. Making flutes is difficult, demanding work. Each worker is at his own work table, intent on his own task. He concentrates on what he is doing and seldom stops to chat with the other workers.

The job of making a flute starts with tubing of whichever metal is used. The tubing is cut into the proper lengths for the

The silver tubing is cut to length—the first step in making a flute.
Photograph courtesy Wm. S. Haynes Co.

The tubing is carefully inspected for defects.
Courtesy W. T. Armstrong Co., Inc.

three sections of the flute. Each flute factory uses slightly different section lengths, though the assembled flutes are always the same length, 26⅝ inches.

A flutemaker buffs and polishes these tubes. He makes them smooth and shiny. At the same time he checks for defects in the metal.

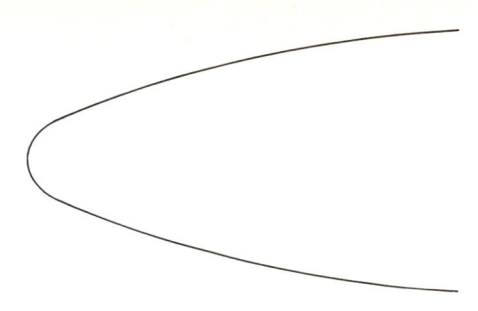

The head joint is formed into a parabolic curve simliar to the one shown here.

The tubing of the head joint gets special treatment. The tube, ¾ of an inch in diameter, is actually a fraction of an inch wider at the end that goes into the body of the flute. The inside of the tube of the head joint is shaped into a parabolic curve.

It takes a very gifted maker to form the head joint. It also requires great skill to place and shape the mouth hole in the

The head-joint tubing is given exactly the right shape in this crucial operation. *Photograph courtesy* W. T. Armstrong Co., Inc.

head joint. The worker makes measurements accurate to a thousandth of an inch, and only the most experienced makers do this job.

Another worker solders the lip plate in place. He measures the hole and plate. If the measurements are not exactly right, he corrects the mistake by hand. The tone of the flute is produced here. A faulty size or placement of the mouth hole can mean that the flute will never sound good.

Highly skilled craftsmen put the tone holes in the body and foot tubes. They use a special machine that follows a master pattern for placing and punching the holes.

Most flutes have drawn tone holes. The shoulder of the hole, the metal that goes around the holes, is drawn up from the metal of the tube. In some of the more expensive flutes, the maker solders a separate shoulder in place. Sometimes the

Final shaping of the mouth hole is done by hand.
Photograph courtesy W. T. Armstrong Co., Inc.

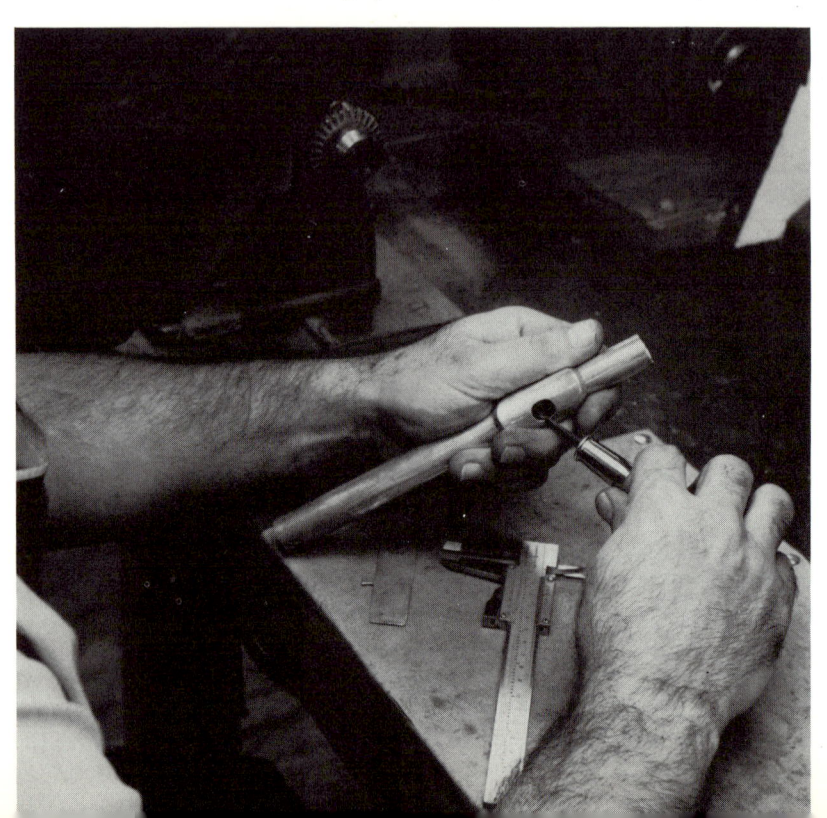

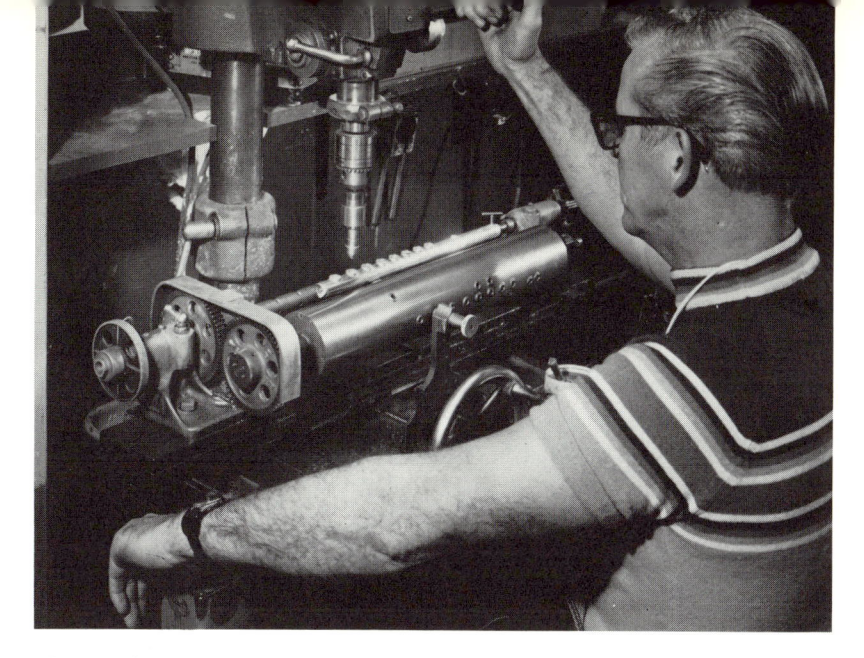

This worker uses the machine to roll the shoulders of the tone hole socket. *Photograph courtesy* W. T. Armstrong Co., Inc.

metal at the top of the shoulder is rolled over, forming a lip all around the socket.

On modern flutes the holes remain open until they are closed by a finger or a key. The keys on a flute are connected to rods that are held by posts attached to the flute.

On the finer flutes, a skilled craftsman finishes the tone holes by hand. *Photograph courtesy* Wm. S. Haynes Co.

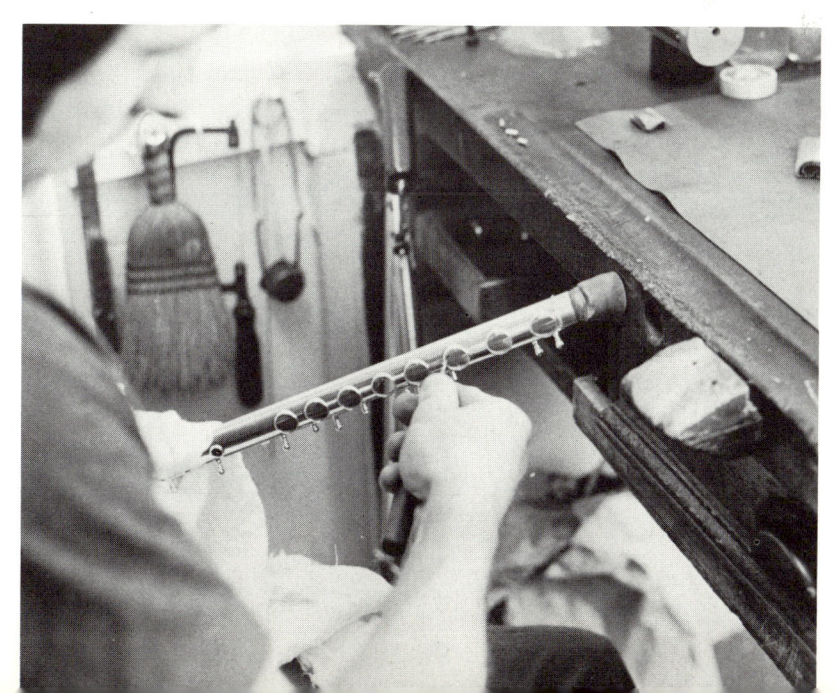

A worker solders the posts to the ribs.
Photograph courtesy W. T. Armstrong Co., Inc.

Usually, the maker solders the posts to ribs. A rib is a thin strip of metal that is curved to match the shape of the flute tube. He uses silver solder to attach the entire rib, with the posts firmly in place, to the tube. These ribs add strength to the tubing, and prevent possible damage to the wall of the flute.

The ribs are filed by hand to make a perfect fit.
Photograph courtesy Wm. S. Haynes Co.

While some craftsmen work on the flute tubes, putting in the mouth hole, making the tone holes and shoulders, soldering the posts and ribs, and engraving the name of the maker on the flute, other workers make the keys.

The player uses the keys to open and close the holes on the flute. He presses on a key to open or close holes that he cannot reach or that are too large to be covered by a finger.

The keys are usually made of the same metal as the rest of the flute. Almost all flutes today use forged keys. The worker places a rough cutout of the metal key in a drop-forge, or press. The forge bears down on the metal with a force of about 100 tons and presses it into the right shape. Forged keys are very strong and usually last the lifetime of the flute.

The maker's name is engraved on every flute.
Photograph courtesy W. T. Armstrong Co., Inc.

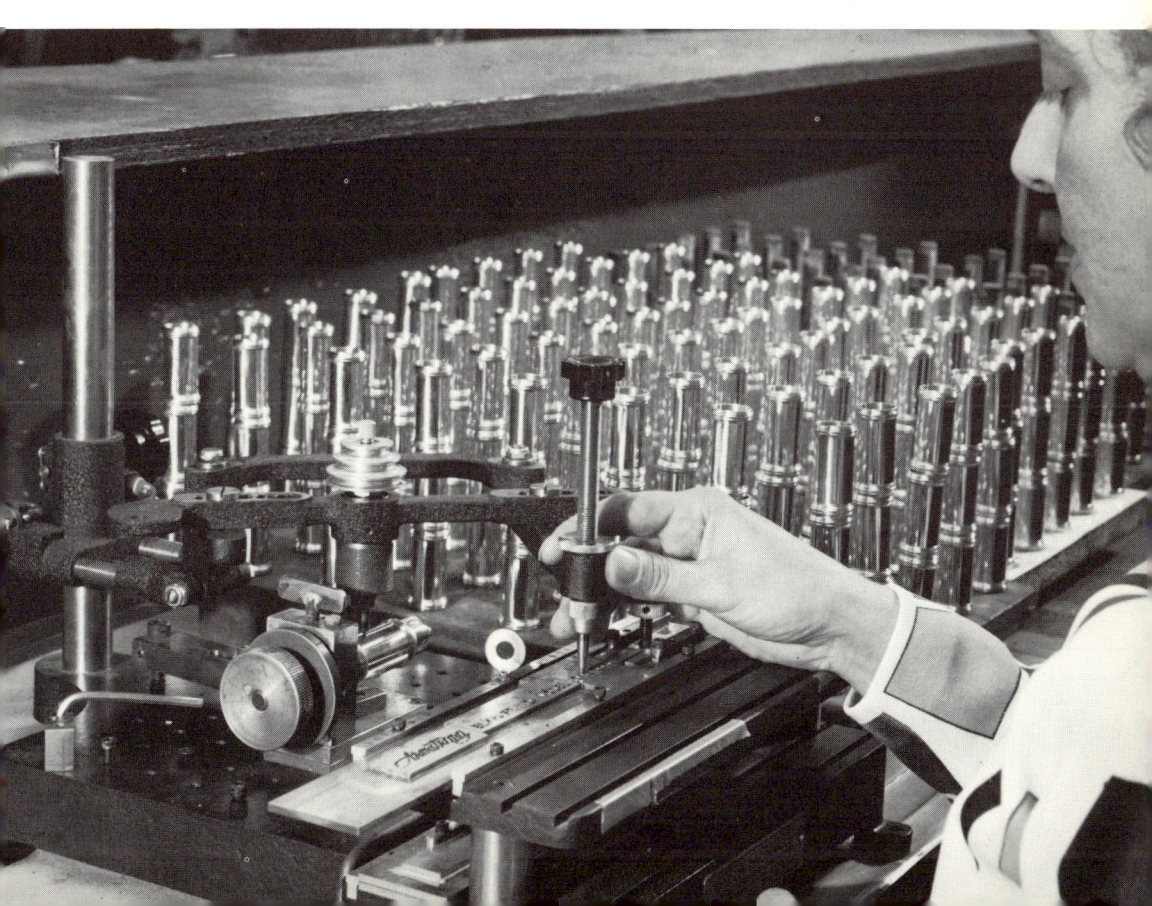

A rough cutout of the key is placed in the die to be shaped by the drop forge.

Photograph courtesy W. T. Armstrong Co., Inc.

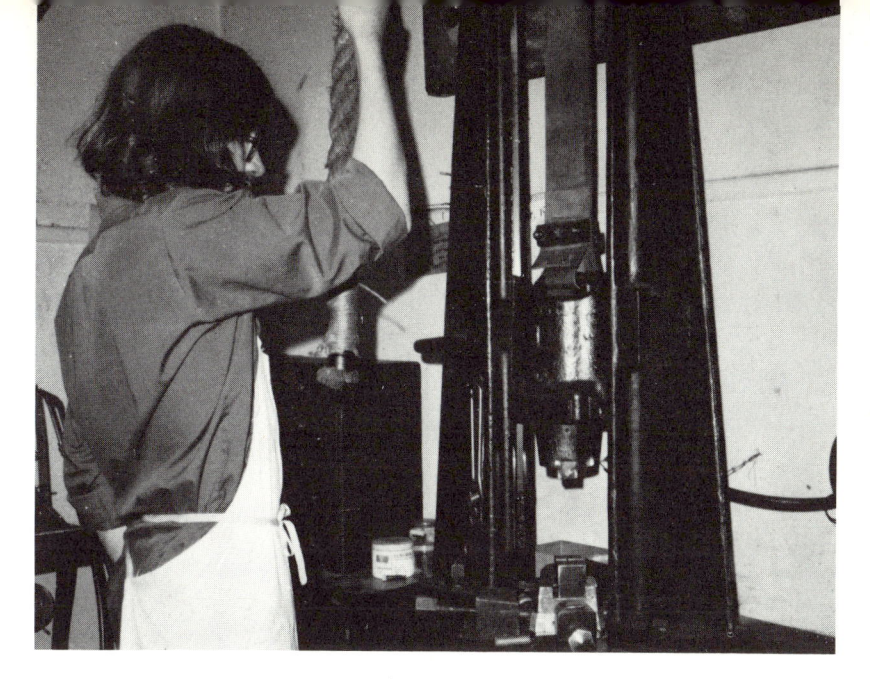

Although this drop forge weighs only 50 pounds, it strikes the key with a force of 100 tons. *Photograph courtesy Wm. S. Haynes Co.*

The tubing and keys of the nickel-silver flutes are then dipped into a bath of liquid chemicals. In this process, called plating, the flute parts are covered with a very thin coat of either nickel or silver.

This worker dips the nickel-silver keys into a chemical plating solution. *Photograph courtesy W. T. Armstrong Co., Inc.*

Now another worker places a pad inside the cup of each key. The pad is made of a circle of felt with a cardboard backing that is covered with either thin plastic or animal bladder skin. He attaches each pad with a dab of sealing wax, a plastic insert, or a screw-washer.

Putting the pads in the key cups is delicate, exacting work.
Photograph courtesy Wm. S. Haynes Co.

It takes many years of training and experience to learn how to fit the keys to the flute. *Photograph courtesy Wm. S. Haynes Co.*

Some flutes, called open-hole, or French models, have some special keys. These keys do not have cups or pads. The player uses his finger to cover the holes. About 80 percent of the professional flutists use open-hole flutes. The tone on open-hole flutes is more brilliant, and some high notes can be played more in tune.

The assembler brings together all the parts of the flute. He collects the tubing, the keys and pads, and the rods that have been prepared by other workers. On his workbench he has the needle springs that will keep the key open over the holes, and the screws that will connect the keys and rods to the posts.

The assembler puts all the separate parts together. He checks himself at every step to make sure that the parts fit well and work smoothly. The assembler is held responsible for the finished flute.

The assembler makes sure all the parts fit well and work smoothly.
Photograph courtesy W. T. Armstrong Co., Inc.

The tester, wearing gloves, plays the finished flute to make sure it sounds good and plays easily.
Photograph courtesy W. T. Armstrong Co., Inc.

The flute then passes from the assembler to the tester. The tester is both a flutist and a craftsman. He plays the finished flute. He listens carefully to the sound and tests all the mechanical parts. His ears and fingers tell him at once if anything is wrong. And he knows enough about flutes and flute making to be able to suggest how it can be fixed.

The tester sends all perfect flutes on for final polishing. The gleaming flute is then packed in its case, which will protect the flute on the way to the music store and for the rest of its life.

The flute gets a final polishing.
Photograph courtesy Wm. S. Haynes Co.

FLUTE MUSIC

An amazing amount of music has been written for flute. There are flute sonatas, which are played either by flute and piano or flute and harpsichord. Outstanding among these are the six sonatas by Johann Sebastian Bach and the twelve sonatas by George Frideric Handel. François Couperin, George Philipp Telemann, and Antonio Vivaldi also composed well-known flute sonatas at about the same time.

These sonatas, written about 250 years ago, usually have four movements. The first and third movements are in a slow speed, or tempo, and the second and fourth movements are usually in a fast tempo.

Not too many flute sonatas were written between the time of these sonatas and the twentieth century. But now composers have again begun to write for the flute. Among the most popular modern flute sonatas are those by Paul Hindemith, Sergei Prokofiev, Walter Piston, Francis Poulenc, and Bohuslav Martinu.

There are a number of outstanding concertos for flute accompanied by orchestra. Wolfgang Amadeus Mozart wrote two well-known flute concertos. Antonio Vivaldi, Georg Philipp Telemann, Giovanni Battista Pergolesi, Carl Philipp Emanuel Bach, Johann Joachim Quantz, and Jacques Ibert are other composers of flute concertos. The *Suite for Flute and Strings*, by Johann Sebastian Bach, is similar to a concerto in that it features a solo flute accompanied by a string orchestra.

Besides the sonatas and concertos there are vast numbers of other solos for flute. A list of a few of the most popular solos includes Claude Debussy's *Syrinx*, Charles Griffes's *Poem*, Howard Hanson's *Serenade*, and Kent Kennan's *Night Soliloquy*.

Finally, the flutist has a large number of important parts in orchestral music. Among the works featuring the flute are the "Chinese Dance" and "Dance of the Mirlitons" from Peter Ilytch Tchaikowsky's *Nutcracker Suite*. (The mirliton is a flute-like instrument, somewhat like a toy flute or kazoo.) The flute is prominent as the bird in *Peter and the Wolf*, by Sergei Prokofiev. It is also featured in Claude Debussy's *Prelude to the Afternoon of a Faun,* Felix Mendelssohn's *Midsummer Night's Dream Music*, Igor Stravinsky's *Petruschka*, and Wolfgang Amadeus Mozart's opera, *The Magic Flute*, to name just a few.

PICCOLO

Piccolo is the Italian word for little. The piccolo is the little flute. It is higher in pitch than the flute. In fact, it is the highest-pitched member of the orchestra or band.

The piccolo is about half the length of the flute. The flute is 26⅝ inches long; the piccolo is 12½ inches. In theory, the piccolo should be exactly half as long as the flute. It is a little shorter because it does not have a foot joint.

Since the piccolo is about half the length of the flute, it sounds an octave, or eight notes, higher than its sister instrument. Music for the piccolo is the same as music for the flute, but the notes on the piccolo sound an octave higher.

Piccolo makers have experimented with the shape of the piccolo tube from the time it was first developed in the late eighteenth century. Today some players prefer conical piccolos, in which the head joint is cylindrical (the diameter is the same throughout), and the body is conical (the diameter narrows towards the open end). Other players choose the cylindrical piccolos, with conical head joints and cylindrical bodies.

Unlike modern flutes, many piccolos today are made out of wood. The usual wood for piccolos comes from the granadilla trees that grow in the Congo area of Africa. The wood is a type of ebony, dark-brown in color, and so heavy that it does not float in water. It is chosen for piccolos because it is extremely durable and crack-resistant, and can be polished to a very attractive high gloss. Most professional piccolo players prefer these wooden instruments.

Some piccolos are made of either silver or nickel silver. Others are made of both wood and metal, usually with a metal head joint and a wooden body. Some very popular students' piccolos are now made of a special plastic. Each maker chooses the materials he feels will produce the best tone, be easiest to play, and be most in tune.

The piccolo is part of most orchestras and bands. Usually one of the flute players also plays the piccolo. The clear, high notes of a single piccolo can easily be heard above the loudest and largest orchestra or band.

Beethoven was the first important composer to write orchestral parts for the piccolo, in his *Fifth* and *Ninth Symphonies*. Among the best-known piccolo parts in band and orchestra music are the solos in John Philip Sousa's "Stars and Stripes Forever" and Tchaikowsky's *Fourth Symphony*. The most famous solo works for piccolo are the three piccolo concertos by Antonio Vivaldi.

ALTO FLUTE AND BASS FLUTE

Flute players have always wanted an instrument that would allow them to play down to lower notes. There were many attempts through the history of the flute to build larger flutes

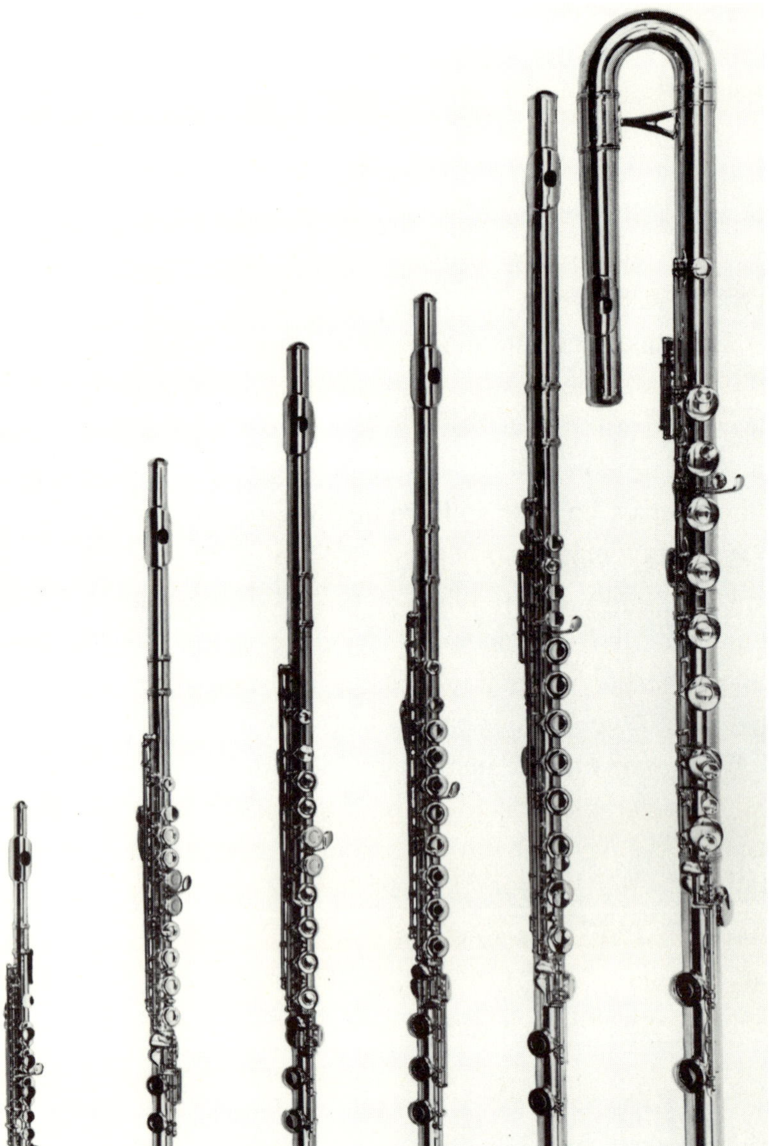

that could play lower. The first practical larger flute was built around 1830 by Theobald Boehm, the father of the modern flute. It is called the alto, or G, flute.

The alto flute plays four notes lower than the standard, or C, flute. It uses the same music as the standard flute, but sounds four notes lower because it is about eight inches longer. The keys on the alto flute are arranged so that the fingers do not have to stretch any more than they do on the standard flute.

There are very few works, or even parts, for the alto flute. A few French composers, such as Maurice Ravel, use the instrument in an occasional orchestral work. There are a few modern works for flute ensembles that have parts for the alto flute. It is not heard very often, but when it is used the alto flute lends a very rich, exotic sound to the orchestra or band.

The most recent member to join the flute family of instruments is the bass flute. The first practical bass flutes were not made until about 1930. The bass flute, which reads the same notes as the standard flute, sounds an octave lower.

To play the low notes of the bass flute, the tube must be over 47 inches long. That is much too long to be held in the ordinary way. Therefore, bass flutes are made so that the tube bends over itself, in a shape called a U-bend. In this way the player can cover all the keys without strain.

Composers write only small parts for the bass flute, and use

The six members of the flute family: piccolo, standard flute, standard flute with B foot, E-flat flute, alto flute, and bass flute. In this photograph all of the instruments are closed-hole flutes except for the standard model with a B foot, which is an open-hole, or French, flute.
Photograph courtesy W. T. Armstrong Co., Inc.

the instrument only for special effects. It has a very distinctive tonal quality, but it is very difficult to play in the lower part of its range.

There is a famous story about a bass-flute player who was hired to go on a concert tour of Europe with an American orchestra. He was told that he would be needed only for one concert. In Paris the orchestra would do a piece that had a short, but important, part for bass flute. The entire part had only three notes: A flat, D, and C.

The orchestra crossed the ocean and performed in city after city. The bass-flute player went along, but he did not have anything to play in any of the concerts. Finally, they got to Paris. His big moment had come at last. He got ready. The conductor signaled, and he played the first note, the A flat. It sounded good. He went down to the next note, the D. It was very soft and could barely be heard. And the last note, the low C, was so soft that no one was able to hear it!

The standard flute, the piccolo, the alto flute, and the bass flute are the four basic members of the flute family. In addition, the E-flat soprano flute is sometimes used. This instrument is about 4 inches shorter than the standard flute, and therefore plays a few notes higher. Also, some of the standard flutes are made with a longer foot joint. Since the extra length allows the standard flute to play one note lower, to B, this model is called a standard flute with a B foot.

SOME STRANGE FLUTES

Some primitive tribes in South America, India, and parts of Asia have a flute that is played by breathing out through the player's nose, instead of through his lips. This nose flute, as it is called, is made from a hollow reed, and is usually about 15 inches long, with four or five finger holes. Quite often the nose flutes are painted bright red. The player keeps his right nostril closed and breathes into the flute through his left nostril only.

Over the years a few flute makers have made flutes for left-handed players. These are mirror images of the standard flute, and are held to the player's left. The fingering is exactly the opposite of that of the normal flute.

Among the most interesting of all flutes are those made for one-armed flutists. Two well-known one-armed flutists played in the early years of the nineteenth century. Carlo Sola, a composer and flutist, had lost his right arm in an accident. Count Rebsomen, an amateur flutist, had lost his left arm and right leg while fighting in Napoleon's army.

Their flutes were specially designed to be played with one arm. There were extra keys to make up for the fact that the player had fewer fingers to use. And the end of the flute had a long post, which the player rested on a table while he played.

CHAPTER THREE

Science and the Flute

A shiny, glittering modern flute is a beautiful work of art. It is also a remarkable, scientific sound producer.

The flute sound is created at the mouth hole in the head joint. The entire tube of the flute then makes the sound louder, and gives the tone its special quality and character. The pitch is raised and lowered by opening and closing the holes along the tube.

You hear sound when something vibrates, or shakes back and forth very quickly. You hear the sound of a violin when the string vibrates. You hear a drum when the drumhead vibrates. And you hear a flute when the column of air inside the tube vibrates. The vibrations set the air around the instrument into vibration. The vibrations travel out as sound waves to your ear.

You can watch vibrations in a simple experiment with a ruler. Hold a wooden or plastic ruler over the edge of a table. Hit one

Science and the Flute 🎵 55

end. The rapid up-and-down movements of the ruler are vibrations.

When the ruler moves up, the air particles above the ruler squeeze together and the air particles below spread out. When the ruler moves down, the air particles below the ruler are squeezed together and the air particles above spread out. Vibrating air particles squeeze together and spread apart hundreds or thousands of times a second.

The air particles in the flute vibrate the same way. When you blow into the flute, your breath is cut by the edge of the mouth hole. Some of the air goes into the tube and sets the air column inside the flute into vibration.

The air particles in the vibrating air column rush back and forth, squeezing together and spreading apart at great speeds. For example, the slowest vibrations are for the lowest note on the flute, C. The air particles vibrate back and forth 256 times a second to produce that note. The fastest vibrations are for the highest note, C, three octaves above the low C. It vibrates at a speed of 2,024 vibrations per second.

The ruler will vibrate and make a sound after you hit it and set it into vibration. *Photograph by Melvin Berger*

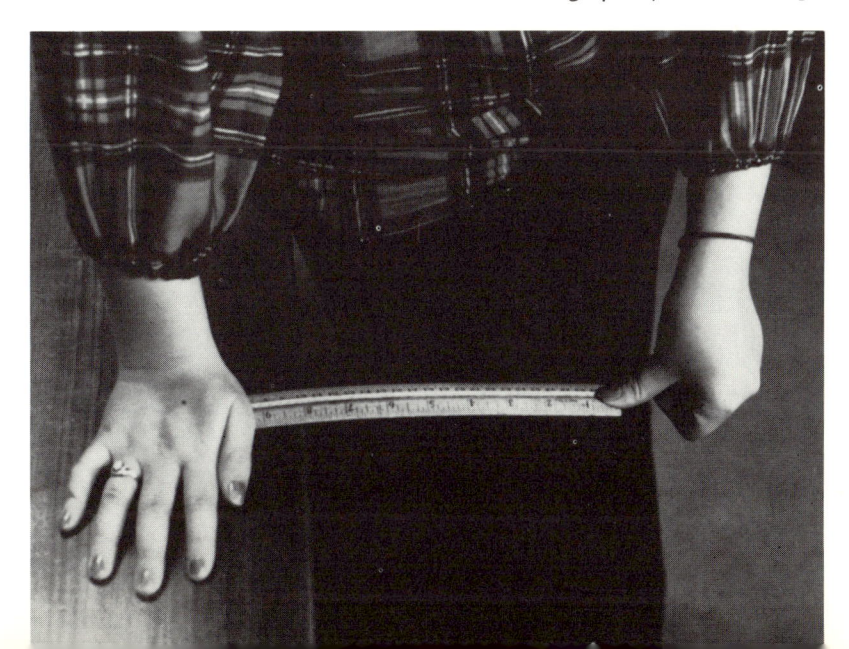

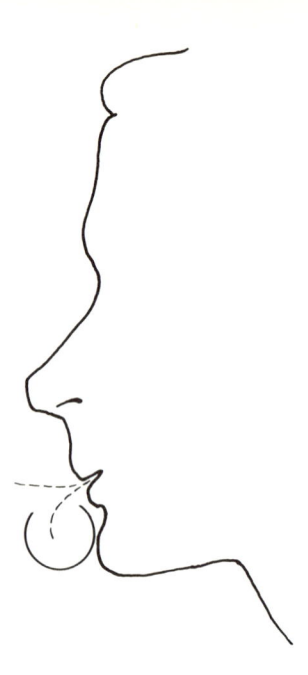

When you blow into the flute, your breath is cut by the edge of the tone hole, setting the air inside into vibration.

But don't get the idea that the air particles rush up and down the length of the flute tube. The air particles are just pushed a tiny fraction of an inch one way or the other. Each particle, though, pushes the particle next to it, sending the vibrations through the entire tube.

Vibrations travel through the tube of a flute like a locomotive that rams into a train with many cars. Each car bumps the car next to it, but no car moves very far itself. One scientist figured out that each air particle at the end of the tube moves back and forth only about twenty-thousandths of an inch for the note A played medium loud.

There is a way to make the air inside a flute vibrate without even blowing into the flute. Tap the flute keys sharply. This sets the air inside the flute into vibration. Do you hear the faint sound made by the vibrating air particles?

The pitch of the flute depends on the length of the vibrating column of air. The shorter the tube, the higher the pitch; the longer the tube, the lower the pitch.

Try this experiment to show how pitch is determined by length. Hold a 12-inch ruler over the edge of a table. Keep 2 inches on the table and let 10 inches extend beyond the edge. Hit the ruler and listen to the pitch it produces as the 10-inch length vibrates.

Now slide the ruler so that 4 inches are on the table and 8 inches extend. When you hit it now, only 8 inches will be able to vibrate. Do you expect the pitch to be higher or lower? It will be higher because the vibrating length is shorter. Try holding the ruler so that different lengths extend. Listen to the changes in pitch that come from changes in vibrating lengths.

You can try this same experiment with a vibrating column of air, instead of a vibrating ruler. Make a sound by blowing across the top of an empty soda bottle. Your breath is cut by the edge of the top of the bottle, setting the air column inside the bottle into vibration. Remember the pitch of the sound you produce.

Now put about 3 inches of water into the bottle. The water makes the column of air inside shorter. Blow again. Do you hear a higher pitch? You might try filling several bottles with different amounts of water. Add enough water in each bottle to make the notes of a scale. Then try to play some simple songs, blowing into each bottle for the note you need.

The very first flutes could play only one note. No one knew how to change the length of the vibrating column of air. In the pipes of Pan there were tubes of several lengths tied together. The player got different pitches by blowing on the different pipes.

Today flute players can change the length of the vibrating

The empty bottle produces a lower pitch than one with water because water shortens the column of vibrating air.

Photograph by Melvin Berger

column in two ways. They can push the head joint farther into the body or pull it out, making the tube a fraction of an inch shorter or longer. When the tube is shorter, all the notes go up slightly in pitch; when the tube is longer, all the notes go down slightly in pitch.

Flutists change the length in this way when they tune up before they play. They do it to match the flute's pitch to the pitch of the piano or the other instruments in the orchestra or band.

Flute players can also change the length of the vibrating

column of air by opening and closing the holes along the tube. They do this while they are playing and going from note to note.

When you close all the holes, the vibrating column is as long as it can be. That gives you the lowest note on the flute. When you open the last hole along the tube, the air escapes at that point, the vibrating column becomes shorter, and you go up one note. As you open each hole, the pitch goes up another note.

That is the basic scientific principle on which the flute is based. But finding the exact place and size for each hole is more complicated.

Each hole must be a compromise. It is a compromise between the best place and size to make the note most perfectly in tune, to produce the best tone, and to be the easiest for the player to open and close. It took many centuries of development and improvement for the modern flute to reach its present high level of perfection.

The modern flute has sixteen holes. Yet the flute can play thirty-six or more notes. How can a flutist play thirty-six notes using only sixteen holes?

For the first twelve notes of the chromatic scale, from middle C to the next C, it is quite simple. The player merely opens the last hole along the tube, and the pitch goes up to the next note. For a few of the notes, there is no hole in just the right spot. For these notes the player uses cross fingerings.

In cross fingering, the player closes some holes, leaves one or two holes open, and then closes another hole. This lowers the pitch that would normally be produced by the closed holes.

For example, the flutist must use cross fingering to sound the note F sharp, which is halfway in pitch between F and G. With four main holes covered, the flute sounds F; with three holes covered it sounds G. To play F sharp, the flutist covers the three holes for G, leaves holes four and five open, and closes hole number six. This lowers the pitch of the G down to F sharp.

To go up an octave, the player increases the pressure of his breath, and directs it a little higher across the mouth hole. This is called overblowing. He fingers the notes in the same way as in the lower octave. But instead of low C, he sounds high C; instead of low D, he sounds high D, and so on.

To play in the third octave, the flutist increases the pressure even more. He directs his breath even higher. In addition, he opens certain holes that are not open for the notes in the lower octaves. These are called vents. They allow some air to escape at different points along the tube. This helps to create the faster vibrations that are necessary for the high notes in the flute's top octave.

The flute can play up three octaves from middle C. Since there are twelve notes in each octave, the flute can, therefore, play thirty-six different notes. (Some flutists can even play higher, up to F sharp, but these notes are very seldom used.)

The length of the vibrating column of air determines what note the flutist sounds. But what determines the quality or beauty of the flutist's tone?

Everyone agrees that the flutist's embouchure, his breath control, and the placement of the sound are most important in good tone production. Most professional flutists are convinced that instruments made of fine silver, gold, or platinum produce the very best flute sound. Some players hold that the quality of the workmanship on the flute is even more important than the metal that is used.

Modern scientists have reached the point where they can explain how the flute works and why it sounds the way it does. In the future we can expect them to use their scientific knowledge to search for ways that might make the flute an even more beautiful musical instrument.

CHAPTER FOUR
History of the Flute

No one knows who made the first flute, or where or when it was made. But there are some ancient legends on how the first flutes came into being.

Along the banks of many rivers there are tall, thin reed or cane plants growing. When the wind blows through these plants it makes a whistling sound. Perhaps it was this sound that gave early man the idea for the first flute.

Many centuries ago the ancient Greeks created a legend to explain this origin of the flute. The story concerns the god Pan, a happy though ugly man, with horns, a beard, tail, and goat's feet.

Pan loved to chase beautiful women. One day he set out after the goddess Syrinx. Syrinx's sister was watching. Just as Pan was about to catch the goddess, her sister changed Syrinx into a reed growing on the riverbank.

History of the Flute ⚜ 63

Pan heard the beautiful sounds of the wind blowing through the reeds. He cut down several lengths of reed and tied them together. As he blew across each reed, it produced a different note. Pan was then able to play melodies that reminded him of his lost love, Syrinx.

A statue of Pan showing the pipes of Pan to another god.

These modern pipes of Pan are still played in some areas of Czechoslovakia.

This early flute is called either pipes of Pan, or syrinx. The most popular type of the pipes of Pan has seven reeds tied together in a row. Others had from five to thirteen separate reeds. There are still a few places in the world today where you can find folk musicians who play on modern versions of the pipes of Pan.

History of the Flute 🙢 65

Other wind instruments also probably developed from the pipes of Pan. Among these early instruments were the ancestors of the modern oboe and bassoon. The player blew between two small sections of reed attached to a tube. The two reeds vibrated against each other to produce the sound. In the single-reed clarinet, which came much later, the reed is clamped to the mouthpiece part of the tube, and vibrates against the mouthpiece.

Some people believe the idea for the first flute came to early man when he heard a sound as he blew the marrow out of an animal bone. They point out that the Latin word for flute is *tibia*, which also means shinbone.

These reindeer-bone ancestors of the flute are more than 30,000 years old. They were found in a cave in Czechoslovakia.

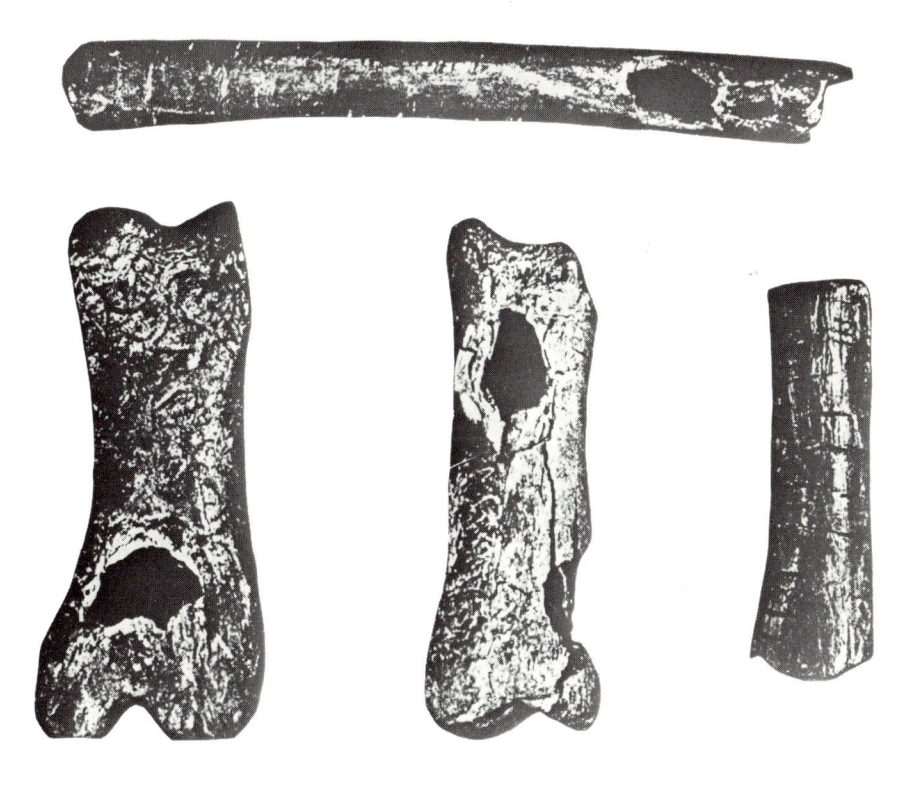

A Greek legend tells us how the bone flute came into being. According to this tale, the goddess Athena made a flute from a deer's horn. As she played it before the other gods she grimaced and made funny faces. The gods laughed at her. In fury she threw the flute away and placed a curse upon the instrument. Anyone who played that flute, she said, would be tortured to death.

According to one legend, the first flute was made from a deer's horn by the goddess Athena, who is represented here by a statue that is nearly 2500 years old.

This carving from about 366 B.C. shows the music contest between Apollo, playing the lyre, and Marsyas, playing the flute. Between them is a servant holding the knife with which he later flayed Marsyas.

Marsyas, a satyr, happened to find the flute and learned to play it very well. He played so well, in fact, that he challenged Apollo to a music contest. They agreed that the winner could punish the loser in any way he chose. At the end, the judges declared Apollo the winner. Apollo had Marsyas tied to a tree and flayed to death. The curse of Athena was fulfilled.

THE MAGIC FLUTE

There has always been an air of magic and mystery surrounding the flute. Certain flute players in the past, and even in modern times, were thought to be able to cast powerful spells by their playing. In different places and at different times the flute has been the symbol of death, of rebirth and fertility, and of love.

In ancient Rome, the flute and death went together. Bands of flutists played at all funerals. When Emperor Nero said, "Call me the flute players!" everyone knew that he had just sentenced someone to death.

Death and flute playing were part of an ancient Aztec ritual, too. Once a year, a handsome prisoner was chosen prince. He was given eight servants and every luxury he might desire. His one duty was to be carried through the street playing the flute, and between melodies, scattering flowers.

Ten days before the year was up, the flutist climbed to the top of the great pyramid. He played his flute four times, facing each of the four directions. All who heard the sound of the flute threw themselves to the ground, prayed to the gods for protection, and at the same time ate a pinch of earth. At the end of the ceremony the flute player was returned to his luxurious quarters.

On the last day of the year, the flutist was brought to the great pyramid once more. This time he carried a large sack of bone flutes. A high priest awaited him at the top of the monument.

The condemned man slowly climbed the steps of the pyramid. At each step he took a bone flute from the bag and smashed it on the stone step. By the top step, all the flutes were gone. Each broken flute symbolized a step toward his approaching death.

At the very top was the altar stone. The flutist bent backwards over the stone. With one powerful stroke of his knife, the priest sliced open the victim's chest. Then, as he prayed and chanted, the priest removed the flutist's heart as a sacrifice to the Aztec god Tezcatlipoca for having allowed the flutist to impersonate the great god of evil and destruction.

Indians living on the Prince Alexander Mountains of New Guinea believe that listening to a flute is harmful to women. At certain times of the year the men of the tribe play their flutes and accompany themselves on drums in a ceremony that lasts all night. They use the magic of the flute to make their sons tall, strong, and fearless. But the women of the tribe are forbidden to see or hear the flutists.

The Greek philosopher Plato held a similar view. He said that if a woman heard a flute player she would lose her goodness. Flute playing should be against the law, he believed, since it had such a powerful effect on women.

The Carib Indians of South America use the flute to announce the arrival of a man in a village. In New Guinea, the Mundugamor Indians trade flutes for wives. And in New Zealand there is a mountain with the wonderful name—*Taumatawkakatangihangakauotanenuiarangikitanatahau*—which means, "The hill upon which Rangi sat and played the flute to his lady love."

PRIMITIVE FLUTES

The story of the origin and early history of the flute is rich in folklore and legend. In recent years, though, music scholars have been able to collect many facts and much information on the early days of the flute. Primitive flutes and pictures of flutes that are thousands of years old have been unearthed. By studying these ancient remains, the scholars can piece together the real story of the flute.

The earliest flutes, called straight-blown flutes, were held in front of the player's face, like the modern clarinet or oboe. The modern flute, which is held across the player's face, is called a cross-blown, or transverse, flute. It came later.

The oldest fragment of a flute was dug up in France some years ago. Scientists estimate that it was made of baked clay about 27,000 years ago. It was a straight-blown flute.

The oldest complete flute was found near Armant, Egypt, during a dig by the English archaeologist, Sir Robert Mond. This flute, which is over two-thousand years old, was made of bronze. It is about one foot long and about half-inch in diameter. There are three holes to change the pitch. It is a straight-blown flute, and probably had a wooden mouthpiece, which was not found. When a modern recorder mouthpiece was fitted to the bronze tube, it was easy to play this primitive flute.

Another flute, the Egyptian *nay*, is believed to be even older, going back some six thousand years. No examples of these early

This three-hole clay flute is similar to the 27,000-year-old flute found in France.

A copy of a painting from a four-thousand-year-old pyramid in Egypt shows three musicians playing the *nay*, which is believed to date back about six thousand years.

nays have been found. But scholars are convinced that the modern *nay*, which is still played in Egypt today, is similar to the primitive instrument.

The *nay* is made of hollow cane, about 1 yard long and ½ inch wide, with two-to-six finger holes. The player holds the *nay* on a slant across his body. He blows across the top of the instrument. His breath is set into vibration by the sharp edge of the top of the cane.

The first mention of a cross-blown flute was in a Chinese poem written about 900 B.C. The Chinese flute, made of hollow bamboo, was called a *ch'ih*.

The earliest picture of a cross-blown flute was found not long ago near Perugia, Italy. It was unearthed in a tomb that was built in the second century B.C. Inside the tomb was a clay urn. On the urn was a carving that pictured a flutist playing a cross-blown flute.

DEVELOPMENT OF THE FLUTE

Over the centuries since these primitive instruments, the flute spread throughout most of the world and was much improved.

By the Middle Ages, the flute was one of the most popular of all musical instruments. There was the straight-blown flute, called a recorder. It was sometimes called a *flûte-a-bec*, which means "beak-flute," since it bears some resemblance to a bird's beak when it is being played. The recorder is quite popular today, since it is rather easy to learn and there is much beautiful music composed for it.

The recorder has a mouthpiece that directs the player's breath past a windowlike cut in the tube. The air is cut by the sharp edge of the window, and set into vibration. The standard recorder has nine holes to change pitch.

The earliest picture of a cross-blown flute was found on a clay urn from the second century B.C.

During the Middle Ages, the recorder was called a *flûte-a-bec*, shown here in a fourteenth century painting.

For a long time the recorder was the instrument for all church music and serious music in general. The cross-blown flute was used mostly for dancing and other popular types of music. When a composer wrote music for flute, he meant for it to be played on a recorder. If he wanted a cross-blown flute to be used he specified *traverso*, which is the Italian name for the cross-blown flute.

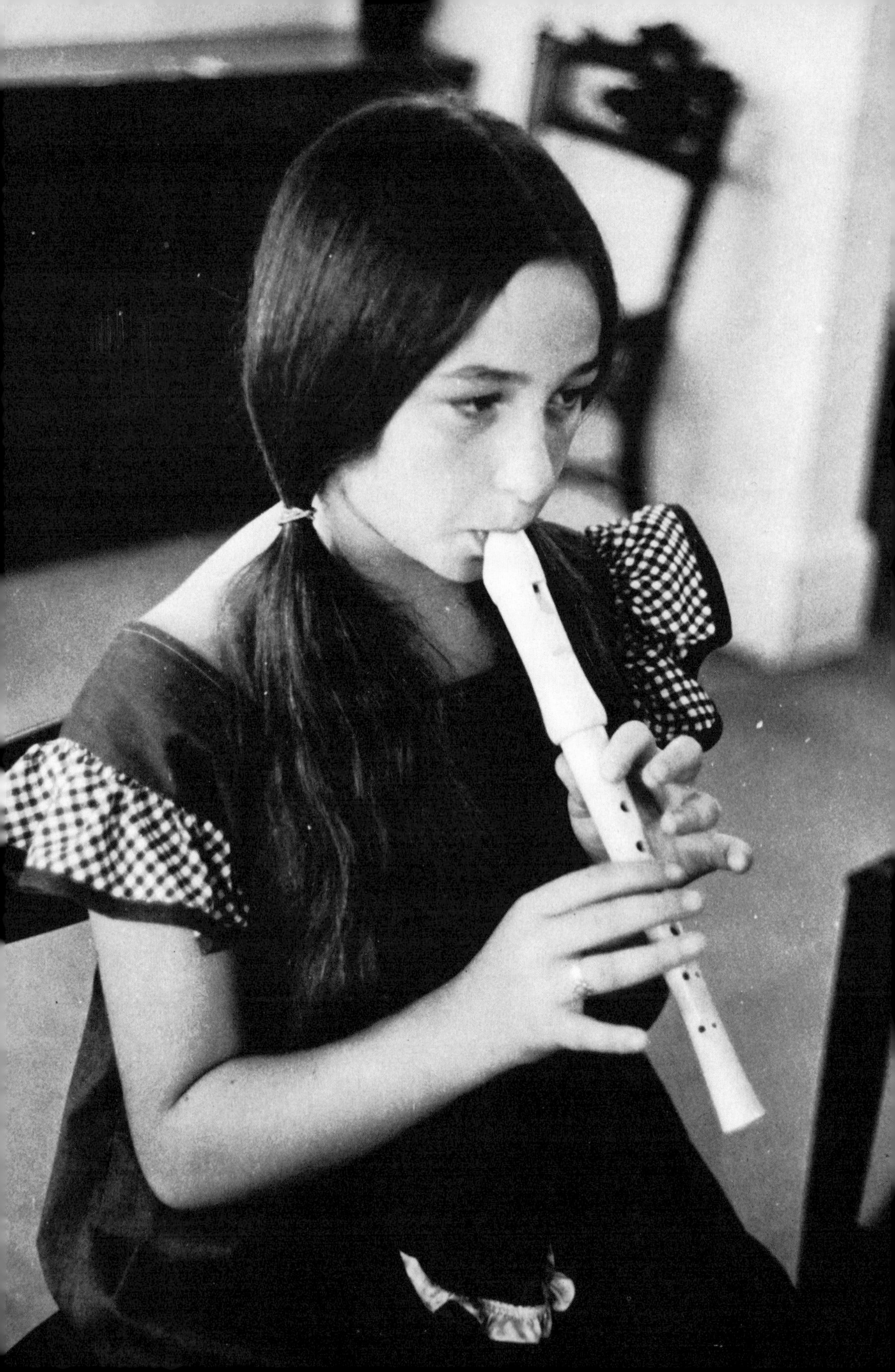

In some places the cross-blown flute is also referred to as the German flute, since it first came to prominence in Germany. The first full description of the Medieval cross-blown, or transverse, flute appeared in a German encyclopedia of the early twelfth century. It described a one-piece, wooden instrument with a plug that closed off one end. There were six finger holes and a mouth hole. By the thirteenth century, the flute was a favorite instrument of the troubadours, the aristocratic poet-musicians of the Middle Ages.

Another type of cross-blown flute from the Middle Ages is the fife. The fife first appeared in the thirteenth century, and quickly became one of the most often used instruments for military music. It has a loud, piercing sound, and is sturdy enough to stand up through rough use. The typical fife is about thirteen inches long, made of wood all in one piece, with a narrow cylindrical tube. It has a mouth hole and six finger holes.

You can hear the fife today in fife-and-drum marching bands that play for military organizations and parades. The modern fife has a slightly wider tube than the fifes of the Middle Ages. But in most other ways it resembles the typical flutes of four and five hundred years ago.

By the year 1650, the cross-blown flute had become somewhat standardized. It was made of wood, usually boxwood, with ivory bands for protection and decoration. Boxwood was chosen because it has a tight, even grain, it has an attractive yellow color, and it is a heavy wood that does not crack easily.

The flute of this time was made in one piece, with six finger holes, no keys, and a round mouth hole. The tube itself was

Although the recorder dates back to the Middle Ages, it is still a popular instrument today. *Photograph by Melvin Berger*

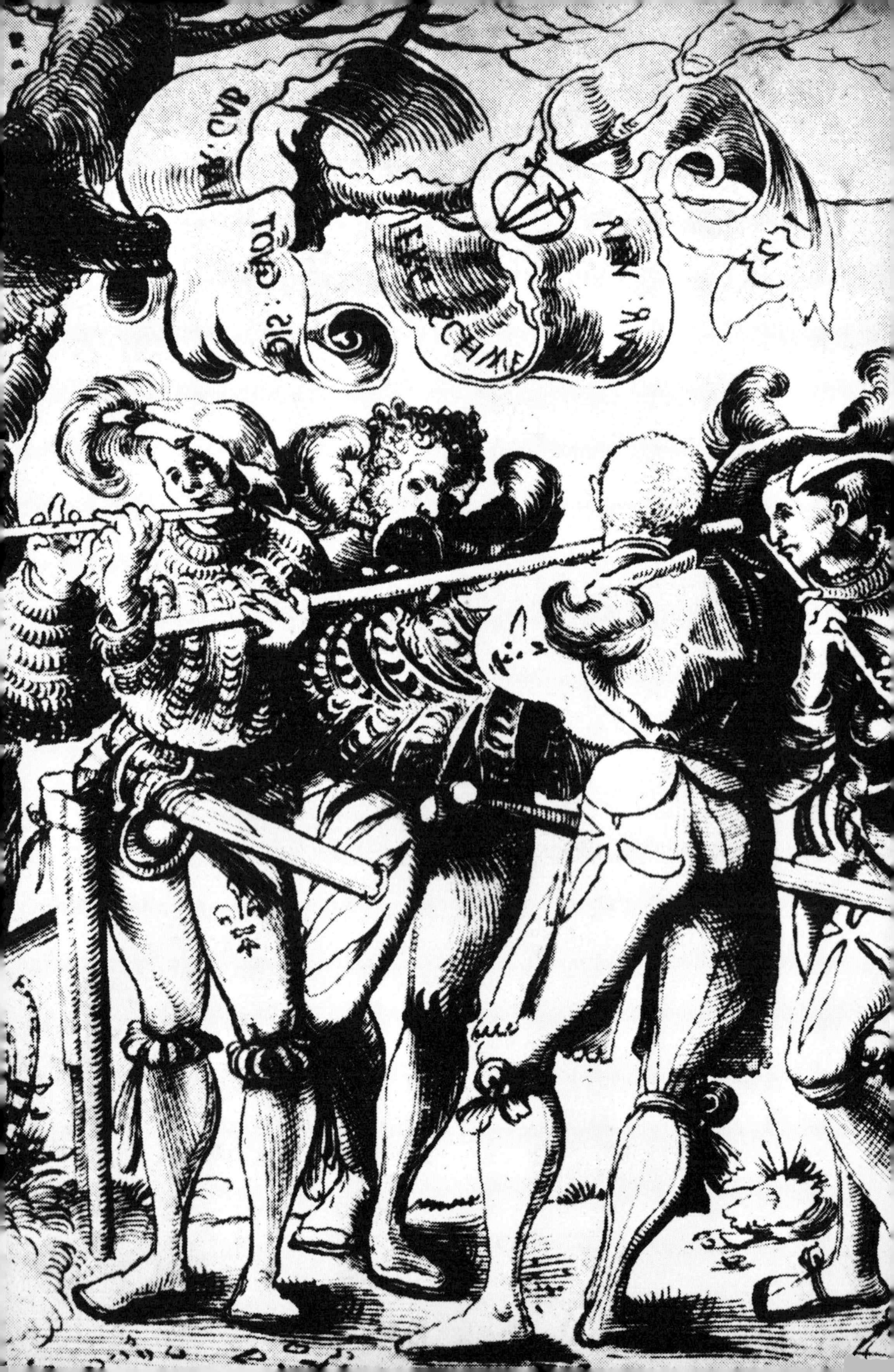

Musicians perform in the private chapel of the Duke of Bavaria. The flutist is shown holding his instrument to the left—probably the artist's mistake.

A sixteenth century German print shows flutes of different sizes being played.

The fife has a high-pitched, penetrating sound; it is often used for parades and military music.   *Photograph by Melvin Berger*

roughly conical, growing slightly narrower from the head to the foot.

The flute sound, though, was rather weak and often out of tune. The finger holes were placed where the player could reach them, rather than where they needed to be to produce a good tone and proper pitches. Since the holes had to be covered by the player's fingers, they were smaller than they needed to be for the best sound. Flute players and makers started to look for ways to improve the flute.

During the next fifty years, from 1650 to 1700, there was great experimentation in flute design. The shape and size of the

The figure standing in the center is Michel de la Barre, one of the leading French flutists of the early eighteenth century. The man seated in the foreground is holding a typical one-keyed flute of that period.

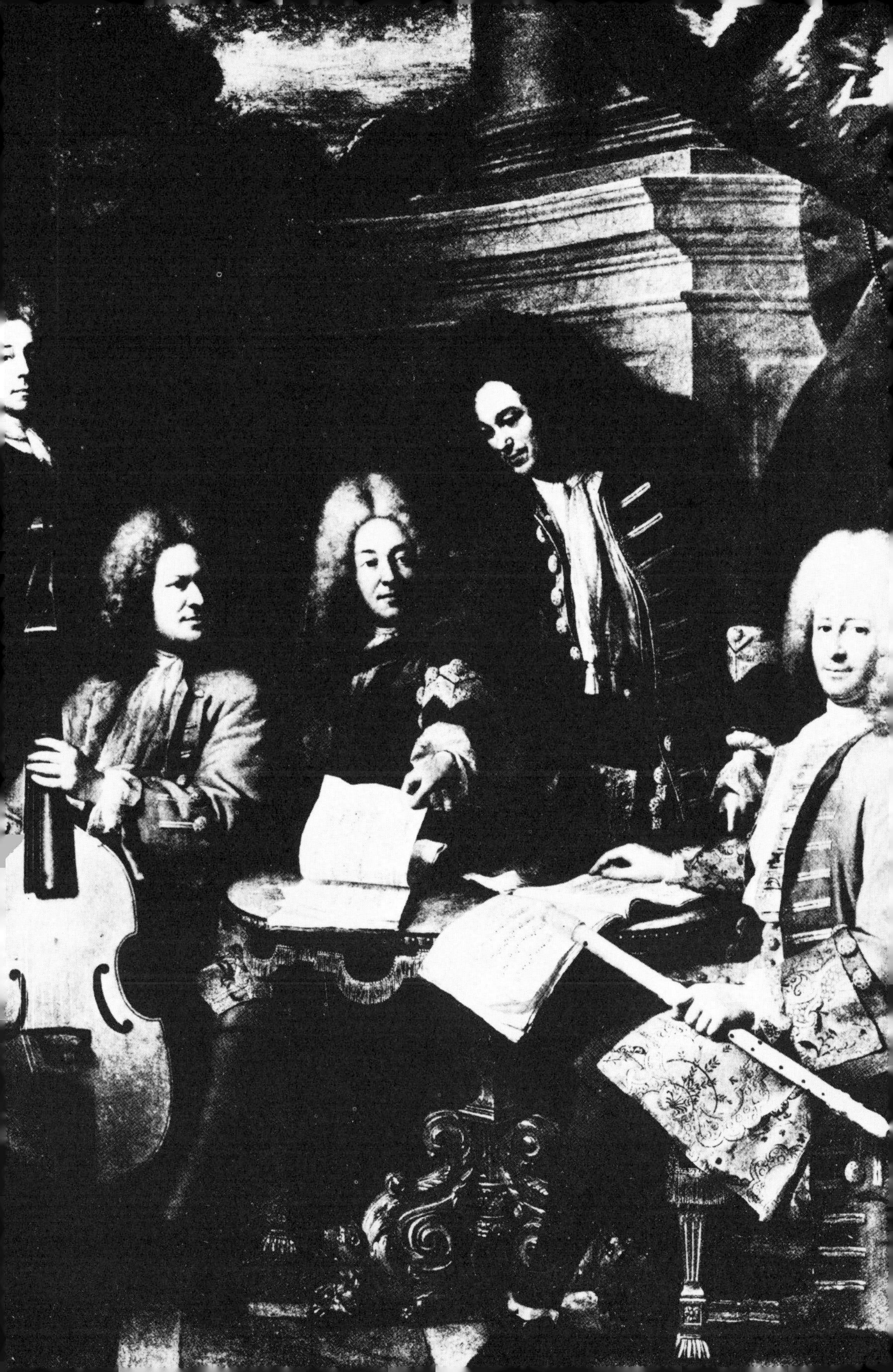

bore, or inside of the tube, was changed. More finger holes were added. There were holes of different sizes. Some makers began using a key to close a hole beyond the player's reach.

Out of this experimentation, a new cross-blown flute emerged. It was designed by Jacques Hotteterre, *la Romain*, of France. (See Chapter 5, Flute Makers, for more about Hotteterre.) The new flute was a big improvement in every way over the older instrument. It was so much better, in fact, that the cross-blown flute began to replace the recorder. Composers began to write music just for the cross-blown flute.

Probably the first orchestral part written for the cross-blown flute was in the ballet *The Triumph of Love* (1681) by the French composer Jean Baptiste Lully. Many, many other composers wrote for the cross-blown flute over the following years, including the two greatest composers of the period, Johann Sebastian Bach and George Frideric Handel. Flutes became so popular that the band of the Gentleman's Concerts in Manchester, England, for example, had no less than twenty-six flutes!

Flutes in orchestras, bands, and solo concerts kept growing during the eighteenth century. Also, large numbers of amateurs learned to play the flute. It is not unusual to see a father holding a flute in the family portraits painted at that time. The list of well-known amateur flutists of the eighteenth century includes poets and writers like Lord Byron, James Boswell, Oliver Goldsmith, and Heinrich Heine. In addition, the philosophers Jean Jacques Rousseau and Arthur Schopenhauer, Noah Webster, who compiled the dictionary, and Giovanni Casanova, the famed Italian adventurer, also played the flute.

One amateur flutist of the time, John Jacob Astor, used the

This illustration from Hotteterre's book shows the flute he designed.

flute to help build his fortune. Astor was born in Germany, where he played the flute as a hobby. When he emigrated to America in 1783, he brought all of his possessions with him, 25 dollars, an extra suit of clothes, and seven flutes.

Soon after his arrival Astor went to the tribal lands of the Seneca Indians, north of New York City. He played his flute and gave them presents of his extra flutes. The Indians accepted him as a trusted friend. They agreed to hunt and trap for him, and to provide him with animal skins and furs. Astor started a very profitable and successful fur business with the help of the Indians he had wooed with the flutes. He went on to become one of the wealthiest men in the United States.

Although the flute flourished throughout the eighteenth century, there were still problems with the tone and playability of the instrument. Flute makers and flute players continued to search for ways to improve the instrument.

By the early years of the nineteenth century there was a bewildering assortment of different kinds of flutes. There was an extra long cylindrical flute with an added foot-joint. There was a very short conical flute with an extremely wide bore at the open end. Flutes could be found that had from six to twenty-one finger holes arranged in many different patterns on the tube. And there were flutes that had from one to eight keys.

Also, there were flutes of different materials. The standard material was wood, and almost every flute until recent times was made of wood. In fact, the flute is still known as a woodwind instrument, even though most flutes today are made of metal. But the other materials that were tried at the time were ivory, glass, leather, cane, pottery, marble, and various metals.

Some good results came out of all this activity. With the

added holes it became possible to have a hole for each note of the chromatic scale (the white and black notes on the piano). Before this the flutist had to use cross fingerings for many of the notes and these were often badly out of tune. There was the beginning of a key system to cover the holes the player could not reach, and to make playing easier. And instead of the leather strips that had been used to cover the holes, new stuffed pads were attached to the keys.

The early stuffed pads were made of thin kidskin filled with wool. Most of these pads were white, but in England all of them were black. The custom of English funeral directors at this time was to furnish black kid gloves to the mourners at funerals. Since the gloves were worn only once, the thrifty funeral directors sold the used gloves to instrument makers, who cut them up and used them to make stuffed pads.

Various flute makers in the early years of the nineteenth century argued and bickered over whose instruments were the best. Each one kept developing his own approach and tried to win others to his way of making flutes. These makers were not interested in learning from each other. They also did not apply the new knowledge of science, especially the science of musical sound, to the design of their instruments.

Then, in 1847, Theobald Boehm designed the best flute of the time. He pulled together all the important advances in flute making, added his own original improvements, and applied the latest scientific thinking to the problem of building an excellent flute. The tone of the new Boehm flute was most beautiful, the notes were all much more in tune, and the system of holes and keys was sensible and efficient. His flute was easier to learn and easier to play than any of the others.

The superior Boehm flute did not result in more interest in the flute, oddly enough. In fact, interest in the flute waned during the nineteenth century. Even though composers still wrote beautiful flute parts in their orchestra music, they hardly wrote any sonatas or concertos for solo players. And very few flutists during that time were known as outstanding performers.

It was not until the twentieth century that the flute again rose to its previous heights of popularity. Composers began writing solo works for the flute, excellent flute players began giving recitals and concerts all over the world, and large numbers of students and amateurs started playing the flute for the sheer joy of mastering the instrument. Today the flute is firmly established as one of the leading instruments of our time.

CHAPTER FIVE
Flute Makers

According to legend, Pan and Athena were the first flute makers. But no one knows the names of the countless men and women who cut the reeds, carved the bones, baked the clay, and shaped the wood of the primitive and ancient flutes.

The oldest signed flute that we have was made by C. Rafi, who lived in Lyons, France, from 1515 to 1553. It is a wooden cylindrical flute that has six finger holes and a mouth hole. It can be seen at the Royal Conservatory of Music in Brussels, Belgium.

There were many makers turning out flutes in the sixteenth and seventeenth centuries, but most of their names are not known. Jacques Hotteterre, *le Romain*, who died in 1761, is the first-known maker to influence the development of the modern flute. (He was called *le Romain* because he spent several years in Rome, Italy.)

The Hotteterre family originated in the village of La Couture-Boussey in the Normandy section of France. Instrument making was an important local craft. The modern French instrument-making firms of Louis Lot, Buffet, and Thibouville all trace their origins back to the same town.

Jacques Hotteterre, *le Romain,* was a member of the band of musicians in the court of the King of France, Louis XIV, known as the *Grande Ecurie.* Several generations of the Hotteterre family played in this group. The *Grande Ecurie* was made up of the leading wind, drum, and violin players of Europe. Many were fine instrument makers as well. They were very well paid and highly respected for their skills in all branches of music.

Jacques Hotteterre, *le Romain,* outstanding flutist and best flute and bagpipe maker of the *Grande Ecurie,* designed and built a new and much improved flute in 1697. The Hotteterre flute, as it is called, became very popular and led to great interest in the flute during the eighteenth century.

The flute was made of wood and had either three or four sections. The head was cylindrical; the body, conical. There was one key to cover a hole beyond the reach of the fingers. The holes were more carefully placed than they were in the older flutes, and some were drilled at an angle to make them easy to reach and to sound more in tune.

Another flutemaker who was active at the time of Hotteterre was P. J. Bressan. Bressan was born in France but moved to England around 1683 and lived there until his death in 1735. The Bressan flutes that are in existence today are copies of the Hotteterre model. They are very elegantly made instruments. The Bressan flute that can be found in the Victoria and Albert

Museum in London is made of ebony wood with a delicate inlaid design of silver.

Tebaldo Monzani was an English flutemaker who opened his workshop in London in 1790. He built many instruments that contributed a great deal to flute design. Perhaps his greatest contribution was the introduction of pads that were held in place in the keys by a screw-and-washer arrangement.

Several flute makers working in the early 1800's made other important discoveries and improvements. C. Laurent, the French flute maker, found a better way to attach the posts to the body of the flute. He used this invention on a flute made of cut glass that he patented in 1806. It was an ornate instrument, with silver bands to protect the glass, and several jewels set into the end of the head joint.

In Stratford, England, the Reverend Frederick Nolan patented a ring key in 1808 that could be used on any wind instrument. The ring key is a thin metal ring that circles a tone hole. It is connected by rods with other keys. When the player presses the ring key, the other connected keys go down at the same time. In this way a single finger closes more than one hole at a time.

That same year another Englishman, Charles Townley, devised a way to use the player's left thumb to lengthen or shorten the tube while playing. If a note was too high, the player could lengthen the tube and lower the pitch. If a note was too low, the player could shorten the tube and bring it up to pitch. Townley also invented a clip-on mouthpiece to direct the player's breath to the edge of the mouth hole. Although neither of Townley's inventions were ever accepted, he is considered a significant flute maker.

A young flutist plays a wooden English flute made in 1830, just before Boehm started his work to improve the instrument.

Photograph by Melvin Berger

Charles Nicholson, an English flute maker, made one very important change in the flute, which has been adopted by all flute makers. Nicholson reversed the trend of making finger holes smaller and smaller that had started with Hotteterre. He made immense finger holes on his instruments. Nicholson flutes had a brilliance and power that most of the earlier flutes lacked.

THEOBALD BOEHM

Theobald Boehm, who became the greatest of all flute makers, was impressed by the sound made by the large holes that Nicholson used in his instrument. He adapted some of the best ideas of Nicholson and others, added many of his own ideas, and built a flute in 1847 that has never been surpassed. The 1847 Boehm flute is still used as the model for all flutes made today.

Theobald Boehm was born in Munich, Germany, on April 9, 1794. His father, Karl, was a well-known goldsmith and jeweler. He had his workshop in the apartment above the one in which the family lived, and where Theobald was born.

The young Boehm was a very bright boy. He enjoyed finding new ways to solve problems. But he could be very stubborn and often insisted that others do things his way.

As a child Theobald enjoyed making jewelry, so his father set up a small workbench for him in the shop. At first he made jewelry just for fun. Then he was given little tasks to do. By the time he was fourteen years old, his father was giving him some of the most difficult jobs in jewelry making. He finished his schooling at an art school, where he learned to design jewelry. By his midteens, Boehm was an expert jeweler, able to do extremely delicate work with gold and valuable jewels.

As a hobby, Boehm enjoyed playing songs on a penny whistle that he had bought for himself. In time he tired of the penny whistle and purchased a one-keyed flute. He taught himself to play this flute. (This instrument may be seen in the Dayton C. Miller flute collection in the Library of Congress, Washington, D.C.) Before long he moved up to a four-keyed flute. His parents noticed that he had a good ear and a talent for music.

But playing the four-keyed flute was not satisfying for Boehm. He wanted the flute to sound more in tune and to have a more beautiful tone. He decided that the only way to get a better flute was to build one himself. In 1810, at the age of sixteen, Theobald Boehm built his first flute. It was a copy of his own four-keyed flute, but made with a great deal more care and accuracy.

He now spent all his spare time away from the jewelry shop

playing his flute. Boehm played quite well for someone who was self taught, but it was far from good playing. In fact, his playing was very annoying to one of his neighbors, Johann Capeller, who happened to be the first flutist in the Royal Court Orchestra. One day Capeller met Boehm and said to him, "You, young flute player, I cannot stand your noisy blowing any longer. Come to me and I will show you how it should be done."

Boehm studied with Capeller for two years. He was a serious, hard-working student. He made very rapid progress. Then, one Sunday morning, Boehm played a flute solo in the local church. Capeller heard it, and at Boehm's lesson that afternoon he asked, "Was it you who played the flute solo this morning?"

"Yes," replied Boehm.

"I congratulate you," Capeller said, "but I have nothing more to teach you."

That same year, 1812, Boehm became first flutist at the Isargate Theatre in Munich. He worked as a goldsmith by day and played as a professional flutist at night. This went on until 1818, when Capeller retired and Boehm took his place as first flutist in the Royal Court Orchestra.

Now that he was in the leading orchestra in Munich, Boehm decided to give up his work as a goldsmith. He married Anna Rohrleitner on October 20, 1820, and started a family, which was to include one daughter and seven sons. He studied composing. And he appeared as a flute soloist in Munich and other cities in Europe.

Through all these years, Boehm thought about ways to improve the flute. He was still dissatisfied with the flute he played. He had some ideas on how to make a better one, but no flute maker would listen to him.

In October, 1828, Boehm decided to open his own workshop and make his own flutes. After all, he was a very skilled craftsman as well as a highly accomplished flutist. Perhaps he could use this special combination of talents to make a better flute than the one he was playing.

The first flutes he made in his new workshop were like the standard flutes of the time. They had six holes and eight keys. The only significant difference was that Boehm mounted the keys on metal, instead of wooden, posts. But they still did not have the beauty and richness of tone that Boehm was after.

One day in 1831, while on a concert tour in London, Boehm heard the English flutist Charles Nicholson, son of the flute maker of the same name. He was astounded at the beauty and richness of Nicholson's tone. He learned that Nicholson played his father's flute. Boehm resolved to make a flute that would match the tone of the Nicholson flute.

Boehm returned to Munich and set to work remodeling his flute. He realized that the better tone of the Nicholson flute came from its large tone holes. Boehm built a new flute with large tone holes. His fingers, though, were too thin to cover these large holes. So he had to devise a system of keys and pads to cover the holes.

Boehm made two other important changes in his new flute. He held the keys up by springs instead of resting them on the holes. The player now had to press the key to cover the holes rather than to open the holes, as in the old flutes. And he adapted Reverend Frederick Nolan's ring key to the flute.

In November, 1832, Boehm gave the first of many public performances on his new flute. The flutists in the audiences showed very little interest in the instrument. Boehm was disappointed, but he understood. Most flutists were unwilling to start all over and learn how to play the completely new Boehm flute.

There was one important exception, though. Victor Coche, flute professor at the Paris Conservatory of Music, was most enthusiastic about Boehm's flute. He wrote to Boehm: "I cannot express to you all the admiration I feel every day in studying your magnificent and rich instrument, which will certainly make a very remarkable revolution in wind instruments."

Coche was so happy with the new flute, in fact, that he wanted Boehm to let him manufacture the new flute in France. But Boehm had already agreed to have Clair Godfroy manufacture the flutes in that country, and, therefore, he had to refuse. This made Coche furious. He turned against Boehm, accusing him of stealing the ideas for the flute from Captain William Gordon, a professional soldier and amateur flutist and flute maker. This dispute lasted for many years, and caused much hard feeling and confusion.

Many scholars have studied the Boehm-Gordon controversy. They found that both men applied ideas to flute making that were common knowledge at the time. But it was Boehm who used these ideas to make the first improved, practical flute.

Soon after introducing this new flute, Boehm grew less interested in making the instrument. In 1833, he closed his workshop, even though he continued to play in the Royal Court Orchestra. He now spent his spare time working on other inventions. Boehm discovered new ways to mine iron and to make steel, and he found a new placement for the strings in the piano.

For thirteen years Boehm worked on these other projects, but hopes of further improving the flute were never far from his mind. In 1846, at the age of fifty-two, Boehm decided to return to the problems of the flute—but in a new way. He enrolled at the University of Munich to learn all he could about musical acoustics, the science of sound. Now he would be able to use scientific principles instead of trial-and-error in his search for a better flute design.

Boehm reopened his flute workshop in 1847. In just a few months, he produced a new flute that was considerably better than the 1832 model. Its tone holes were in exactly the right places and of exactly the right sizes to produce the best possible tones, and sound most perfectly in tune. After the holes were set, Boehm built a key system that made it easy for the player to cover and open each hole.

Boehm found that the best shape for the flute tubing was a cylindrical body with a slight tapering of the head joint, in the form of a parabolic curve. This shape gave all the notes a better quality, and made the flute easier to blow.

For the first time, Boehm also began to make metal flutes as well as flutes of wood. Although he made flutes of silver and nickel, he preferred brass for his best flutes.

Boehm's 1847 flute was so much better than any of the other flutes of the time that flutists everywhere began to switch over to the new instrument. It grew more and more popular in every country of Europe and in America. Flute makers began to imitate the design of Boehm's new flute. In fact, Boehm's 1847 flute became the model for all flutes made since then. With only minor changes it is the model for all flutes being made today.

The next year Boehm's eyesight began to fail, and he was forced to retire from his position in the Royal Court Orchestra

—a position he had held for thirty years. He now spent his time teaching the flute.

Boehm, the teacher, worked to improve his students' playing in every way he could. He concentrated, though, on beautiful tone production and quick memorization of music.

Boehm had an especially interesting approach to helping his students memorize. He would give the student a new piece and tell him to play it. When the student finished, Boehm would turn the music upside down and tell him to play it again. The idea was to see how much the student could memorize the first time he played through the piece.

In 1871 Boehm wrote *The Flute and Flute Playing*. This book describes the Boehm flute and gives instructions on how to play it with good tone and style.

He spent a great deal of time composing after his retirement. All in all he turned out about sixty compositions for the flute. A few of them may still be heard at flute recitals.

As he grew older, Boehm's health began to decline. His eldest child, Mary, took care of him until his death on November 25, 1881. Boehm died in the same apartment in which he had been born and in which he had lived for eighty-seven years. He left the world richer for his creation of the modern flute.

Boehm's workshop continued to manufacture flutes under the watchful eyes of Carl Mendler, who had become Boehm's business partner in 1867. Boehm's son, Theobald III, and Mendler kept the shop going from the time of his retirement until 1900. At that time E. L. Leibl took over the firm and produced flutes that were engraved "Boehm and Mendler." When that firm went out of business in 1920, the direct line that began with the Boehm flute of 1847 came to an end.

Theobald Boehm at sixty.

A skilled craftsman in the Haynes workshop files keys by hand.
Photograph courtesy Wm. S. Haynes Co.

MODERN FLUTE MAKERS

Soon after Boehm introduced his 1847 flute, makers in Europe and America began to manufacture instruments modeled on it. One of the leading American flute workshops was set up in 1888 by William S. Haynes. The Boston factory is still making fine flutes. Over the years it has built over forty-thousand flutes and piccolos.

There are skilled master craftsmen at work in the Haynes

factory. Some of these men were trained from five to fifteen years before they were allowed to do the delicate hand work they do. Many machines are also in use. Some, such as the drop forge, were part of the original Haynes workshop. Other machines are the most modern and advanced models that are available.

Each year the Haynes factory builds about eight hundred flutes. But the demand for Haynes flutes is so great that there is a one-and-a-half-year wait for a new Haynes flute.

Another flute manufacturer, the Powell Company, also has a long waiting list. Verne Q. Powell, founder of the company was a jeweler in Fort Scott, Kansas. He was always interested in flutes. As a boy he made a piccolo out of a length of brass pipe. Later he made a silver flute, melting down several silver dollars, seven silver teaspoons, and a silver watchcase to get the silver.

In 1914, Powell went to work in the Haynes factory. Thirteen years later, in 1927, he opened his own factory, also in Boston.

Haynes and Powell flutes tend to cost more than most flutes because there is so much hand labor in their manufacture. The least expensive silver flutes sold by these companies are under 1,000 dollars, gold flutes are about 4,000 dollars, and platinum flutes cost approximately 6,000 dollars.

Most flutes today, though, are made in large factories that depend more on machines than on hand-crafting. By using modern tools and equipment, they are able to turn out large numbers of good-sounding instruments at moderate cost. The flutes made in these factories cost about 200 dollars or more. The best-known flute factories are W. T. Armstrong, Gemeinhardt, Selmer, and Artley.

But whether they are made in a small workshop or a large factory, all flutes today can be traced back to the 1847 model made by that most remarkable of all flute makers, Theobald Boehm.

In the large W. T. Armstrong flute factory, a worker controls a power forge that stamps out flute keys.
Photograph courtesy W. T. Armstrong Co., Inc.

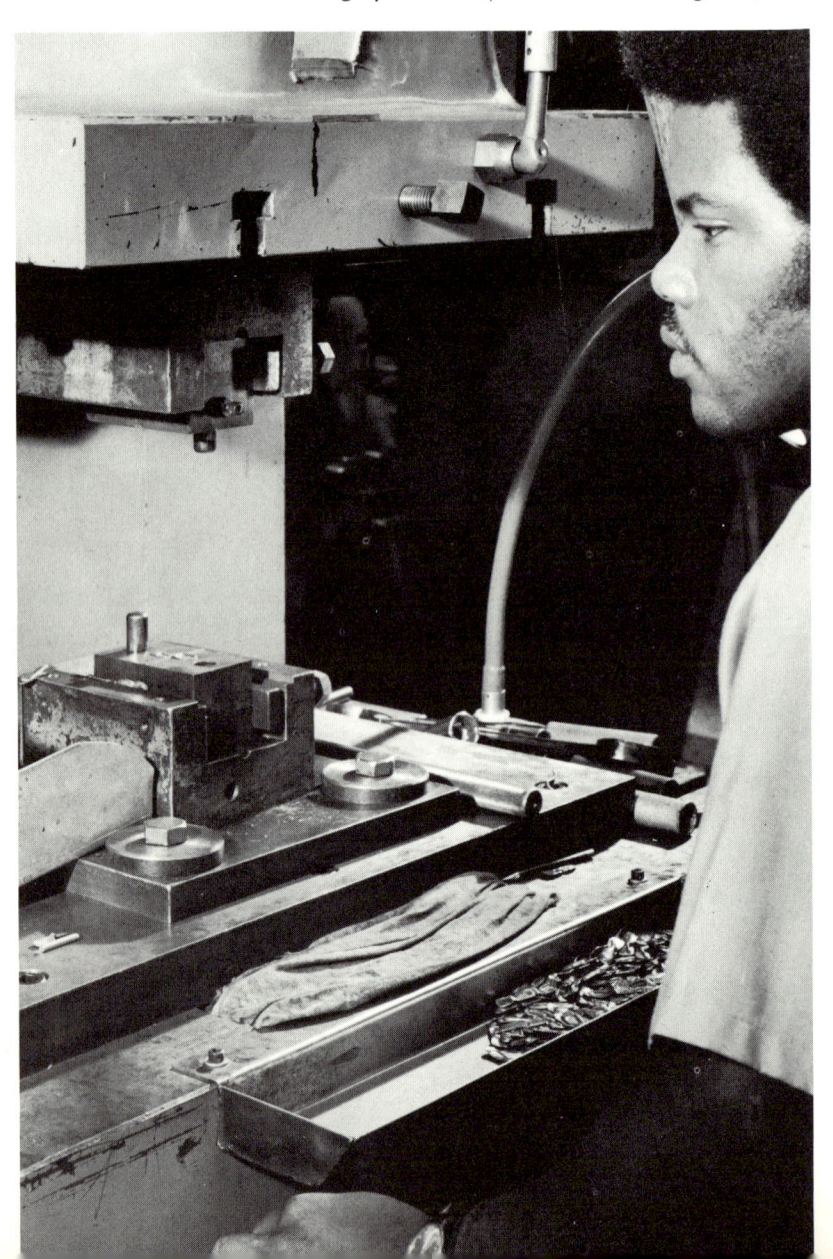

CHAPTER SIX
Flute Players

The flute has been played for thousands of years. But who were the players who played at tribal ceremonies and at village dances? Who played while tending the sheep and for the soldiers who marched off to war? Their names are unknown.

We read that Cleopatra's father played the flute in ancient Egypt. The history books tell us that King Henry VIII of England left seventy-two flutes, seventy-six recorders, and six fifes when he died in 1547. But our information about early flute players is incomplete.

The first performers we know about are a group of French flutists who were very active around the year 1700. The leading player was Jacques Hotteterre, *le Romain*, who is also remembered for his improvements in the design of the flute. Hotteterre devised new methods of holding, blowing, and fingering the flute. He put his ideas into a book, *Rudiments of the Flute,* which was published in 1707. This is the first method book for the cross-blown flute. It set down many of the basic rules of flute playing that are still followed today.

Michel de la Barre, Descoteaux, and Philbert were also well-known players of the same time. Little is known of their lives or ability, but they are described as outstanding players at the French royal court.

Some years after the French group, Pierre Gabriel Buffardin (1690–1768) rose to fame. Buffardin was also a Frenchman, but in 1716 he went to Germany to become the first flutist in the Royal Orchestra in Dresden. Today Buffardin is best remembered as the teacher of the first "star" flutist, Johann Joachim Quantz (1697–1773).

QUANTZ AND FREDERICK THE GREAT

Johann Joachim Quantz was born in Oberscheden, Germany, on January 30, 1697, the son of a blacksmith. At the age of nine, Joachim began to work at the same trade. But one year later, when his father died, the young Quantz was taken in by an uncle, Justus Quantz, who was a musician. His uncle taught him to play various instruments and to compose.

By the age of seventeen, Quantz was earning his living by performing on the oboe and flute in various orchestras. A few years later he gave up the oboe to concentrate on the flute and study with Buffardin. Buffardin and Quantz are credited with creating what is now known as the German school of flute playing.

As his reputation grew, Quantz was asked to give recitals in many countries in Europe. He also spent time in Warsaw, Prague, and other cities, playing in their orchestras. In March,

1728, he settled down as flutist in the well-known Royal Chapel Orchestra in Dresden.

Many notable people attended the concerts given by Quantz in Dresden. One evening the young Prince Frederick of Germany (1712–1786) was in the audience. He had traveled from the Royal Castle in Berlin to Dresden for a visit. The sound of Quantz's playing made a very strong impression on the young Prince. Later that year, when Quantz gave a recital in Berlin, Frederick again went to hear him. The Prince longed to study the flute. He asked his father, King Frederick William I, to let him study with Quantz.

The King agreed. He tried to convince Quantz to leave Dresden and live in Berlin. But Quantz wanted to stay in Dresden. He arranged, however, to make two long visits to Berlin each year, and to give the Prince flute lessons each day of his stay.

The lessons went very well, In fact, from the King's point of view they went too well. The Prince was so absorbed in his music that he did not do such princely things as study politics and military science, and learn to ride, shoot, and hunt. The King became angry with Frederick for the interest he took in the flute as well as in art and poetry. He wanted his son to be a strong military leader and to take charge of the powerful army he had built up. As the King wrote, "Fritz (nickname for Frederick) is a pipe player and a poet. He cares naught for soldiering, and will spoil all my work."

The King tried to turn young Frederick away from the flute. He forbade the lessons. But with the help of the Queen, Quantz and Frederick continued the lessons in secret.

There is a story that one day the King overheard Quantz giving Frederick a lesson. He stormed up to Frederick's room.

Quantz, in a panic, grabbed the flutes and music, and jumped into an empty firewood cabinet. He remained there, trembling with fear, for fifteen minutes while the King stomped about searching for him.

Finally, Frederick could no longer bear the King's demands. The eighteen-year-old Prince decided to run away with a trusted friend. But both young men were soon captured and thrown into prison. The King ordered that Frederick's friend be beheaded, and he forced Frederick to watch the execution. This experience shocked Frederick.

In time, however, Frederick and his father grew closer together, and in 1832 the King gave Frederick his own palace in Rhemsberg. Now he could live as he chose, free of his father. He spent all of his spare time practicing his beloved flute.

Frederick plays for his friends at the palace in Rhemsberg.

During a typical day, Frederick played for half an hour after he awoke, and then got a few extra minutes between the courses of breakfast. He usually practiced twice more during the morning, and once after lunch. He finished most days by performing for his friends in the evening.

When Frederick became King, at the age of twenty-eight, he named Quantz Court Composer. Quantz spent time with the King daily. He played duets with him. He composed new works for the King and other musicians in the Court to play. He made flutes for the King to play on. Frederick's collection of flutes was so large, in fact, that he had one servant whose only duty was to care for them. Quantz also conducted or played when the King performed at the nightly concerts.

Frederick reigned from 1740 to 1760. During those twenty years, he proved to be a most remarkable king. His army was the mightiest in Europe, he reformed the government of his country, and he encouraged and helped bring about advances in science, agriculture, economics, and ways of manufacture.

He also was a most remarkable flutist and composer. Even though he spent a lot of time on military and state affairs, Frederick would find a way to practice the flute each day. In his lifetime, moreover, he composed one hundred twenty-one flute sonatas and four concertos for flute and orchestra. About twenty-five sonatas and all four concertos have been published and are available on records.

How did Quantz correct Frederick when he made a mistake? Once, when Quantz heard Frederick play some wrong notes he cleared his throat very loudly. Frederick caught on. He stopped and corrected his mistake. Then he said, "We must not let this place cause Quantz a sore throat."

Quantz taught Frederick and played with him for thirty-two years. The older man was working on his three-hundredth concerto for flute and orchestra when he died on July 12, 1773, at the age of seventy-seven. He had finished three out of four movements of the work. So close were these two men in thought and love for the flute, that Frederick was able to write the last movement to complete the concerto. This became part of the legacy of compositions for the flute that Quantz left behind. All in all, he wrote twenty-six sonatas for flute and harpsichord, many duets, trios, and quartets, as well as the three-hundred concertos for flute and orchestra.

Frederick played the flute for a few years after Quantz died. But he was troubled by gout, a disease that affected his fingers. In 1779, at the age of sixty-seven, he had to give up the flute. "I have lost my best friend," he said as he put away his flute for the last time.

Frederick's last years were sad and lonely. He was unhappily married, and he and his wife had no children. At the end his closest companions were two greyhounds, which he asked to have buried near him. He died on August 17, 1786. But he lives on in history a brilliant and powerful monarch of the eighteenth century, and a superb flutist and composer.

OTHER EIGHTEENTH AND NINETEENTH CENTURY FLUTISTS

The leading flute virtuoso in the last year of the eighteenth century was Johann Baptist Wendling (1720–1797). He played first flute in the orchestras in various cities of Germany. Wendling was a close friend of the composer Wolfgang Amadeus Mozart, who often asked his advice on writing for the flute.

Two men, Charles Nicholson and Theobald Boehm, also famous for their important work in developing the flute, were popular flutists after 1800. But the flute began to fall from favor. Fewer soloists appeared in public. Little new solo music was composed for the flute.

In fact, during the years from about 1800 to 1900, the flute became the butt of many jokes. The composer Luigi Cherubini, speaking of the out-of-tune playing of many flutists, said that the only thing worse than a flute in an orchestra was two flutes. Antonio Ghislanzoni, who wrote the libretto for Verdi's opera *Aida*, said this about flute players: "The unhappy man who succumbs to the fascination of this instrument is never one who has attained the full development of his intellectual faculties. He always has a pointed nose, marries a nearsighted woman, and dies run over by a bus. The man who plays the flute frequently adds to his other infirmities a mania for keeping weasels, turtle doves or guinea pigs."

But the cruelest thought of all is expressed in his old poem from around the same time:

> Nature gave flute players brain,
> Of this there can be no doubt;
> But alas! it all is in vain,
> For quickly they blow them out!

Then, close to the beginning of the twentieth century, a wonderful change took place. New flutists began to appear, playing with greater skill and beauty than ever before. Composers began to write for the flute. There was such an upsurge of flutists and flute music that the twentieth century is often called the golden age of flute playing.

MODERN FLUTE PLAYERS

Georges Barrère was one of the first major flute players of the twentieth century. He was born on October 31, 1876, in Bordeaux, France, the son of a furniture maker.

When Georges was ten, he was given a toy whistle that his older brother was tired of. He quickly mastered this toy instrument and before long was even teaching this instrument to other students at school. By the age of twelve, he had also taught himself to play the flute.

That same year Georges was sent to a military school, where he was made leader of the school's fife band. His interest in the flute grew, and he started to take lessons. He decided to attend the Paris Conservatory as a music student.

Barrère applied to the Paris Conservatory late in 1889, but was refused. The flute teacher, Henri Altès, however, invited

A famous bust of Georges Barrère made in 1937 by Marion Sanford.
Photograph courtesy Wm. S. Haynes Co.

Flute Players 107

him to listen in on the flute classes and try again the next year. At the age of fourteen, Barrère was accepted as a regular student at the Paris Conservatory.

Just about this time, Barrère had an argument with his family. They cut off all of his funds. He was forced to move into a tiny room in a dingy hotel. He later said that this room was so small that he had "to use my bed for a music stand and to open the windows in order to have the elbow room necessary to secure the correct position of a flute player." To support himself, he played in the orchestras at the Folies-Bergère night club and at the Paris Opera.

Barrère's first years at the Conservatory were not distinguished. He received the lowest possible award for his flute playing. Nevertheless, in his last year, after he undertook studies with the excellent new teacher Paul Taffenel, he was able to graduate with first prize in flute.

For the next ten years, Barrère was very busy as one of the leading flutists in France. He gave recitals, performed in chamber-music groups, and played first flute in major orchestras in Paris. Then an important opportunity came his way. Barrère was invited to come to America and become first flutist of the New York Symphony (now called the New York Philharmonic). He held this job from 1905 to 1928.

During these years, Barrère did more than just play in the orchestra. He also gave many solo recitals and played in many chamber-music groups. Many people flocked to hear Barrère's beautiful playing. Many others were attracted because of his handsome, bearded appearance. Word traveled that Barrère made clever and witty comments at his programs. These comments, made in a very charming French accent, added to the audience's enjoyment. When asked why he never lost his accent, Barrère replied that he took pains to keep it. He felt that he and his accent should never be separated.

As Barrère's fame spread, composers began to write music just for him. One of the most interesting of these compositions is Edgar Varese's *Density 21.5* for solo flute. Barrère had started playing on a silver flute. Later he switched to gold, and then in 1935 he bought a flute made of platinum. *Density 21.5*, which takes its name from platinum's chemical density, was written in honor of the new flute. Barrère played the work at his first concert with the platinum flute on February 16, 1936, at New York City's Carnegie Hall.

Georges Barrère died on June 14, 1944. He had lived to see the flute returned to its place of prominence among musical instruments.

There were other outstanding flutists in the early part of the century. Marcel Moyse, born May 17, 1889, was one of the most influential. Although he spent most of his life in France, he taught and played in America from time to time. He may best be remembered for his teaching. He taught his students to concentrate on the musical content of a composition as a way of developing a good technique, a beautiful tone, and the correct style of performance.

William Kincaid was well known as the solo flutist of the Philadelphia Orchestra from 1921 to 1961, when he retired. In addition, he had a world-wide reputation as an outstanding flute teacher. Kincaid's playing in concerts or on phonograph records of the Philadelphia Orchestra set the standard of orchestral flute playing for several generations of modern flutists. He had an incredible technique and a warm, rich tone. As master player-teacher, he affected almost every leading flutist of our time. Among Kincaid's collection of flutes were the ones that belonged to two famous eighteenth century amateur flutists, Lord Byron and James Boswell.

Perhaps the best-known and most successful of today's flutists is the French virtuoso Jean-Pierre Rampal. He seems to play the flute effortlessly and naturally. His technique is staggering, and he creates the impression that he never stops to take a breath. His tone is lovely. He draws from the flute what he calls "the sound of humanity itself."

Jean-Pierre Rampal was born July 1, 1922, in Marseilles, France. His father, Joseph, was flute professor at the Marseilles Conservatory. Joseph Rampal did not wish his son to be a flutist, and Jean-Pierre did not show any great interest in the instrument as a boy. In fact, he was most interested in painting.

At about thirteen years of age, Jean-Pierre and his family decided that he should head for a career in medicine. But, just for fun, he asked his father to teach him to play the flute.

When it was time for college, Rampal entered the University of Marseilles to study science. At the same time he enrolled at the Marseilles Conservatory to study the flute. In 1937, he received the Conservatory's first prize in flute. In 1941, he received his degree in science and entered medical school. He was going to become a doctor.

The Second World War, however, changed Rampal's mind and his choice of career. While he was in medical school, the German army conquered France and occupied the country. In 1943, during his third year of school, the Germans drafted him into the army.

Rampal was stationed near Paris. He heard that he could get

a two-week leave if he applied for entrance to the Paris Conservatory. He applied to the school.

Rampal played for the flute teacher and was accepted to the Conservatory. Then, just as he was about to report back to the army post, he learned that his unit was being sent to do forced labor in Germany. He decided to run away and hide rather than go to Germany.

At first he hid out in Marseilles and spent his time dodging the police. Then he went to Paris, believing he would be safer there. He met the flute professor at the Conservatory, who suggested that Rampal attend some classes. Rampal agreed, and in five months was graduated with first prize in flute playing.

Germany was driven out of France in 1945. The war was over. Rampal thought about going back to medical school, but finally chose to stay with the flute. "I was," he says, "at least one person for whom the War was a benefit. I can now see that without music in my life, I would have—well, suffocated."

In short order, Rampal took a job as flutist in the orchestra of the Paris Opera, signed up for his first concert tour, made his first recordings, and married Françoise Bacqueryrisse, a harpist.

Almost at once Rampal became internationally famous. Mostly he played the music of the baroque period of music, the time of Bach and Handel. Many music-lovers seemed to be hungry for music from this time. Rampal believed that after the war people wanted "music that was reasonable, ordered, and less emotional—peace after the emotional upheaval of war." He performed these works all over the world. Also, he discovered and played forgotten works of the baroque period, and organ-

Jean-Pierre Rampal is completely absorbed by his music when he performs. *Photograph courtesy of Colbert Artists Management, Inc.*

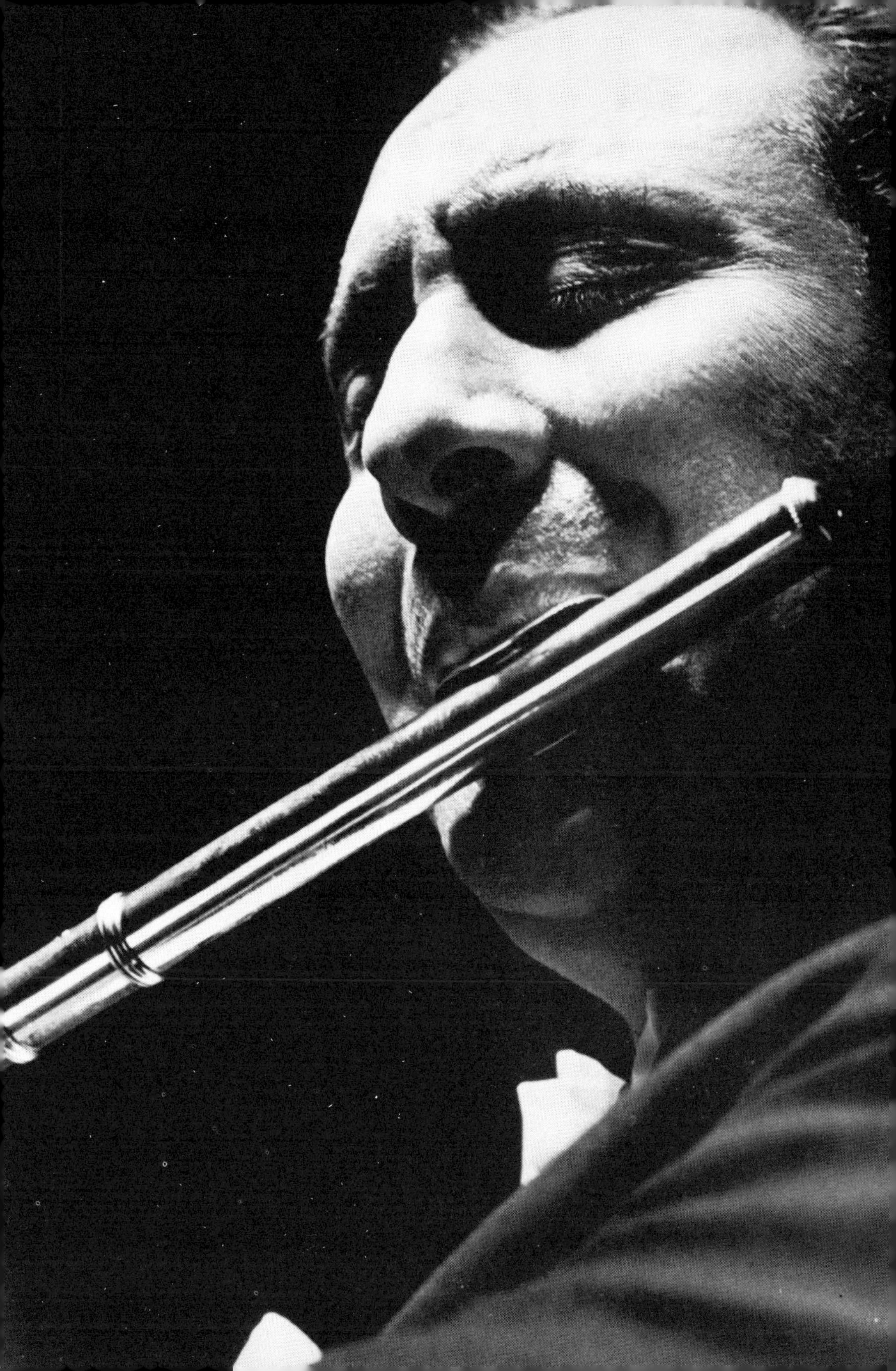

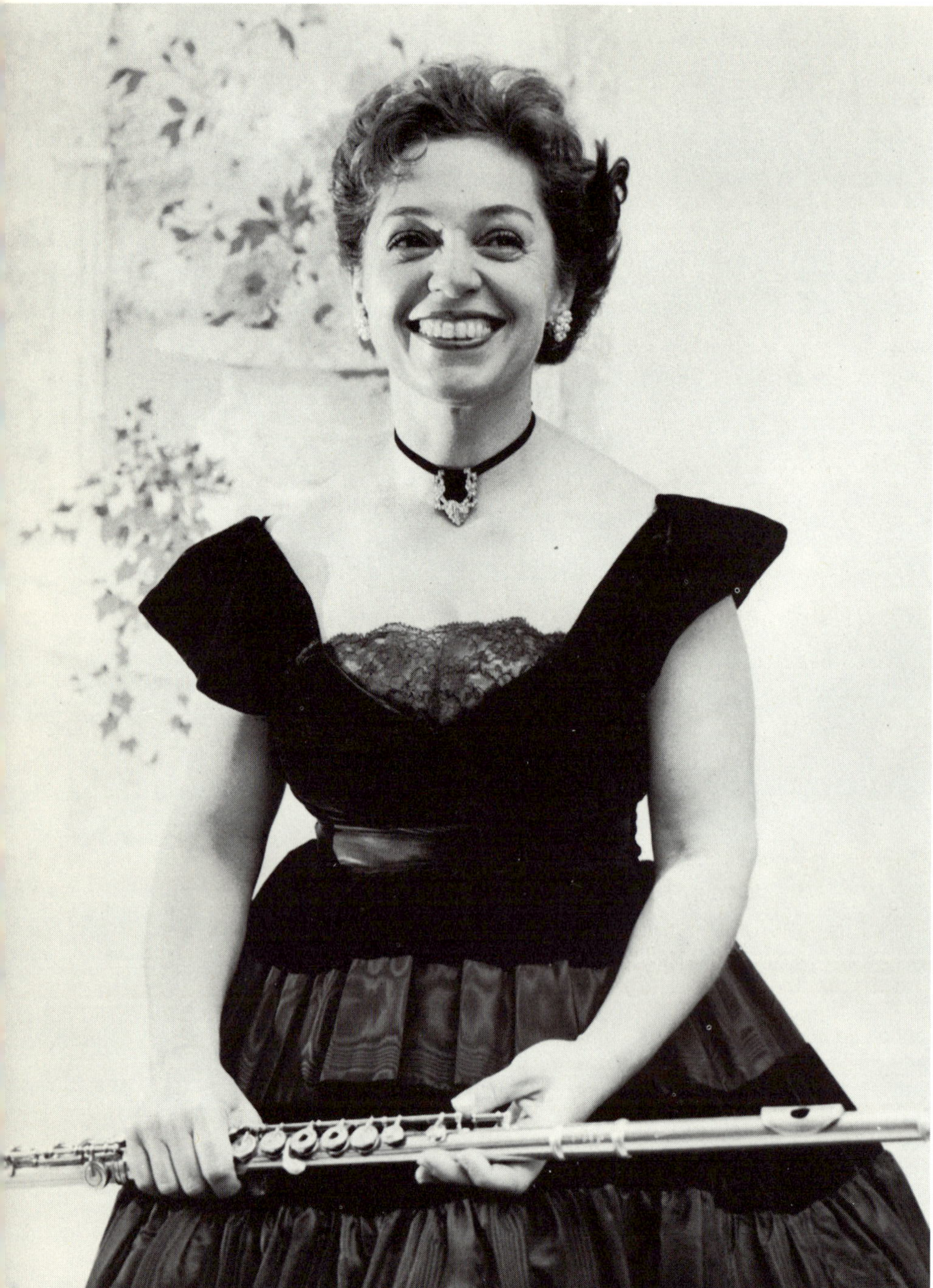

ized chamber groups that specialized in music from the baroque.

Rampal is a large man, over 6 feet tall and weighing more than 200 pounds. When he enters the stage, he fills it with his presence, even though he has a very calm, matter-of-fact stage manner. He usually plays to standing-room audiences that flock to hear him in all the large concert halls and major music festivals throughout the world. In recent years he has been playing modern compositions as well as the baroque works for which he is famous.

But just one great flutist like Jean-Pierre Rampal does not make this the golden age of flute playing. There are many other outstanding flutists who are carrying forward the long and wonderful tradition that belongs to this instrument.

Ruth Freeman, who studied with Georges Barrère, is a leading American flutist. Born in Cleveland, Miss Freeman has been heard in concerts throughout the United States and in many other musical centers throughout the world. She has been a member of several major chamber music ensembles, including the Salzado Concert Ensemble and the New York Concert Trio. During the summer of 1971, she went on a tour with the Traldy String Quartet, performing in churches and cathedrals in England, Holland, Germany, and Belgium.

Miss Freeman's present busy schedule shows her involvement with every aspect of flute playing. She gives recitals and appears as soloist with orchestra. She is first flutist with the Musica AEterna Orchestra. She teaches at the Juilliard School of Music and is founder and director of the Long Island Junior Flute Club.

Ruth Freeman is one of the leading flutists of our time.

Samuel Baron, a distinguished American flute soloist.
Courtesy Sheldon Soffer Management

Brooklyn-born Samuel Baron is in the forefront of flutists. He started his musical studies on the violin, but with the help and encouragement of his high-school music teacher, changed to the flute. After studies at Brooklyn College, he continued with Georges Barrère at the Juilliard Graduate School of Music in New York.

Baron was graduated in 1948 and launched his career. He played in several New York City orchestras, helped to found the New York Woodwind Quintet, and began to appear in recitals.

This young artist was successful wherever he went. He was engaged to tour all over the world with the Quintet; he gave recitals and made recordings of old and new solo flute music; he was hired to teach at Yale and Stony Brook Universities; and he was appointed flutist in the Bach Aria Group.

One of the highpoints of Baron's career came in 1968, when he was invited to play at a festival called "The Art of the Flute," in Rome, Italy. The other two participants were Jean-Pierre Rampal and the Italian virtuoso Severino Gazzelloni.

Baron advises flute students to seek new directions for their careers, to find places where they can make the greatest contributions and derive the greatest satisfactions. He sought and found a new direction when he organized the New York Woodwind Quintet at a time when there were no similar groups.

Among the many other outstanding flutists to be heard today are Paula Robison and Elaine Shaffer. Paula Robison is as well known for her chamber-music performance as for her solo appearances. She is a member of the Chamber Music Society of Lincoln Center and is often heard in joint recitals with her husband, the violist Scott Nickrenz. Elaine Shaffer, born in America and now living in England, does most her concert appearances and recording in Europe.

Many distinguished modern flute players play in orchestras. In almost every city of the world, the best flute players are to be found in the orchestra that performs in that city. Julius Baker of the New York Philharmonic and Doriot Anthony Dwyer of the Boston Symphony have world-wide reputations, both as orchestral performers and solo artists.

It is impossible to name all of the important flutists of our time. The list is too long and it is always changing and growing. Some flutists are well-known only in one city or one country. Older flutists retire and stop playing. Young flutists are entering the field all the time. Some join an orchestra or band; others become members of chamber music groups; a few give recitals in an effort to launch solo careers. Among them are the flutists who become the great leading flute players of tomorrow.

Julius Baker plays first flute in the N.Y. Philharmonic, seen here in a performance conducted by Pierre Boulez.
Photograph by Christian Steiner, courtesy N.Y. Philharmonic

Glossary

Alto flute: Eight inches longer than the standard flute, the alto flute can play four notes lower.

Bass flute: The largest member of the flute family, nearly twice the length of the standard flute, the bass flute plays an octave lower.

Bassoon: The lowest-pitched member of the woodwind family; the tone is produced by blowing through a double reed.

Bore: The hollow space inside the tube of the flute.

Clarinet: A member of the woodwind family; the sound is produced by a single vibrating reed.

Concerto: A composition, usually in three separate movements, for a solo instrument accompanied by orchestra. It is sometimes performed with a piano playing the orchestra part.

Conical: In the shape of a cone, like an ice-cream cone. The diameter of conical tubing grows slightly larger from one end to the other.

Cross fingering: A method of fingering a wind instrument in which the player leaves some holes open between closed holes.

Cylindrical: In the shape of a cylinder, like a tin can. The diameter of cylindrical tubing stays the same throughout its entire length.

Diaphragm: The muscular wall that separates the chest from the abdomen.

Embouchure: The shaping of the lips and tongue to play a wind instrument. Embouchure hole is another name for mouth hole.

Fife: A small, shrill type of flute with six holes that is used mostly in marching and military music.

Flutter tonguing: A wobble in the flute tone caused by a rolling tongue movement.

Key: A metal device, consisting of a cup and a shaft, that is used to cover the holes on the flute. The shaft is connected to a rod; the pad is in the cup.

Mouth hole: A large oval hole in the head joint. The player blows across the mouth hole to produce the flute tone. Also called embouchure hole.

Nickel silver: A shiny metal made of copper, zinc, and nickel that is used to make most of the less expensive flutes.

Oboe: A member of the woodwind family; the sound is produced by a double reed.

Octave: An interval of eight notes, such as from one C to the next C, or from one D to the next D. The higher note vibrates twice as fast as the note an octave lower.

Overblowing: Blowing harder and a bit higher across the mouth hole, causing the pitch to jump an octave higher on the flute.

Pad: The cushionlike part of the key that actually covers the hole.

Parabolic curve: The inner shape of the head joint of the flute. When you throw a ball nearly straight up in the air, it rises and falls in a similar parabolic curve.

Piccolo: The small flute, about half the length of the standard flute, that sounds an octave higher.

Post: The upright supports attached to the flute body that hold the rods.

Recorder: The straight-blown flute that was popular in the past, and is enjoying a revival of interest in the twentieth century. Also called *flûte-a-bec*.

Reed: A type of tall grass with a stiff, hollow stem. The pipes of Pan were made of sections of reed. The reeds of the other woodwind instruments are made of small pieces of reed. Also called cane.

Rib: The thin slightly curved piece of metal to which the posts are attached. The ribs are soldered to the flute body.

Ring key: A thin metal ring around a tone hole that allows the player to control more than one key with a single finger.

Rod: The thin metal bar to which keys are attached; the rods are supported by posts.

Shoulder: The raised metal rim around each of the tone holes on the flute.

Sonata: A composition, usually with three or four separate movements, for one or two instruments. A flute sonata is for flute and piano or flute and harpsichord.

Tone holes: Holes in the body of the flute that are opened and closed to change notes.

Tonguing: The use of the tongue to interrupt the flow of air while playing the flute; tonguing gives each note a clean, sharp start.

Transverse: Passing across or crosswise. It refers to the cross-blown, or modern, flute, rather than the straight-blown flute, or recorder.

Vibrato: A slight wavering or fluctuation of the pitch of a note.

Woodwind quintet: The most popular wind chamber music group, consisting of flute, oboe, clarinet, bassoon, and French horn. Also, music for this combination.

The Flute on Records

COMPOSER	TITLE	PERFORMER	RECORDING COMPANY
Bach. C.P.E.	Concertos	Linde	Deutsche Grammophon
Bach, J.S.	Sonatas	Shaffer	Angel
Bach, J.S.	Suite for Flute and Strings	Rampal	Orion
Beethoven	*Serenade*, Flute, Violin and Viola	Rampal, Jarry, Collot	Decca
Collected	Fifes and Drums	------	Colonial Williamsburgh
Collected	French Recorder Music	Brüggen	Telefunken
Collected	Great Marches	Bernstein, N. Y. Philharmonic	Columbia
Danzi, Franz	Woodwind Quintets	N. Y. Woodwind Quintet	Nonesuch

The Flute on Records

COMPOSER	TITLE	PERFORMER	RECORDING COMPANY
Debussy	*Prelude to the Afternoon of a Faun*	Tilson-Thomas, Boston Symphony	Deutsche Grammophon
Debussy	*Syrinx*	Dwyer	Deutsche Grammophon
Frederick the Great	Concertos and Sonatas	Linde	Deutsche Grammophon
Griffes	*Poem*	Mariano	Mercury
Handel	Sonatas	Debost	Nonesuch
Hanson	*Serenade*	Pellerite	Coronet
Hindemith	Sonata	DiTullio	G.S.C.
Hotteterre	Pieces	Harnoncourt	Vanguard
Kennan	*Night Soliloquy*	Pellerite	Coronet
La Barre	Sonata	Rampal	Dover
Martinu	Sonata	Bryan	Lyrichord
Mendelssohn	*Midsummer Night's Dream Music*	Ormandy, Philadelphia Orchestra	Columbia
Mozart	Concertos	Shaffer	Seraphim
Mozart	*Magic Flute* (Excerpts)	Klemperer, N. Y. Philharmonic	Angel
Mozart	Quartets, Flute and Strings	Dwyer, Silverstein, Fine, Eskin	RCA Victor
Pergolesi	Concertos	Rampal	London
Philidor	Sonata	Rampal	Dover
Poulenc	Sonata	Nicolet	Telefunken
Prokofiev	*Peter and the Wolf*	Bernstein, N. Y. Philharmonic	Columbia
Prokofiev	Sonata	Bryan	Lyrichord

COMPOSER	TITLE	PERFORMER	RECORDING COMPANY
Quantz	Concertos	Barwahser	Telefunken
Quantz	Sonatas	Rampal	Orion
Ravel	*Daphnis and Chloé*	Bernstein, N. Y. Philharmonic	Columbia
Stamitz, K.	Woodwind Quartet	Berlin Philharmonic Winds	Deutsche Grammophon
Stravinsky	*Petruschka*	Boulez, N. Y. Philharmonic	Columbia
Tchaikovsky	*Nutcracker Suite*	Fiedler, Boston Pops	RCA Victor
Tchaikovsky	*Symphony No. 4*	Stokowski, American Symphony	Vanguard
Telemann	Concertos	Rampal	Nonesuch
Telemann	Sonatas	Baron	Dover
Varese	*Density 21.5*	Paris Instrumental Ensemble	Angel
Vivaldi	Concertos	Baker	Vanguard
Vivaldi	Piccolo Concertos	Baker	Vanguard

Index

alto flute, 49, 50, 51, 52

Bach, Carl Philipp Emanuel, 47
Bach, Johann Sebastian, 47, 80
Baker, Julius, 115
band
   amateur, 30–31
   marching, 22
   school, 20, 22
Baron, Samuel, 112–115
Barrère, Georges, 106–108, 112, 114
bass flute, 50, 51–52
bassoon, 22, 24, 65
Boehm flute, 83–84, 92, 93, 94, 96
Boehm, Theobald, 51, 83, 88–94, 98, 105
bone flute, 65–67, 68
Boston Symphony, 115
Buffardin, Pierre Gabriel, 100

chamber music, 24
ch'ih, 71
clarinet, 22, 24, 65
concerto, 25, 29, 47, 103, 104
Couperin, François, 47
cross-blown flute, *see* flute, cross-blown
cross fingering, 59–60, 83

Debussy, Claude, 47
diaphragm, 16, 18
Dwyer, Doriot Anthony, 115

E-flat flute, 50, 52
embouchure, 16, 18, 60
experiments, 54–55, 56, 97

fife, 75
flautist, 12
flute

assembler, 44
body joint, 13, 15
care of, 13–14, 19–20
clubs, 31
cross-blown, 73, 75, 80, 100
double tonguing, 18
factories, 33–46, 96–98
finger holes, *see* flute, tone holes
flutter tonguing, 19
foot joint, 13, 15
French model, *see* flute, open hole
head joint, 13, 15, 35–36, 58
holes, *see* flute, tone holes
keys, 13, 15, 20, 37, 39, 42, 44, 80, 82
lessons, 11–13, 16
lip plate, 36
mouth hole, 13, 15, 35, 39, 54, 55, 60
open hole, 43, 50
orchestral music, 48
origin, 62–67, 69–71
pads, 13, 19, 42, 44, 83, 87
position, 15–16
posts, 37, 38, 39, 44, 87
ribs, 38, 39
ring keys, 87, 91
rods, 13, 15, 37, 44
soloists, 29
solos, 24
springs, 44, 91
tester, 45–46
tone holes, 13, 36, 39, 59, 60, 78, 82, 83, 91
tonguing, 16
trio, 24
tube, 32, 33–35, 36, 39, 41, 44, 54, 58, 75, 78, 82, 93
vibrato, 18

flûte-a-bec, *see* recorder
flutists
  amateur, 30
  chamber music, 28
  professional, 25, 27–29, 43
Frederick the Great, 101–104
Freeman, Ruth, 112
French horn, 24

German flute, 75
Griffes, Charles, 47

Handel, George Frideric, 47, 80
Hanson, Howard, 47
Haynes, William S., 96–97
Hindemith, Paul, 47
Hotteterre *le Romain*, Jacques, 80, 85, 86, 99–100

Ibert, Jacques, 47

Kennan, Kent, 47
Kincaid, William, 108–109

Lully, Jean Baptiste, 80

Martinu, Bohuslav, 47
mirliton, 48
Moyse, Marcel, 108
Mozart, Wolfgang Amadeus, 47

nay, 70–71
New York Philharmonic, 107, 115
Nicholson, Charles, 88, 91, 105
nose flute, 52–53

oboe, 22, 24, 65
orchestra, 25
  amateur, 30–31
  school, 20, 22

symphony, 25, 27

Pan, 62–65, 85
Pergolesi, Giovanni Battista, 47
piccolo, 48–49, 50, 52
   important music for, 49
pipes of Pan, 57, 63–64, 65
Piston, Walter, 47
pitch, 56–60
Poulenc, Francis, 47
Powell, Verne Q., 97
Prokofiev, Sergei, 47

Quantz, Johann Joachim, 47, 100–104

Rampal, Jean-Pierre, 109–112, 115
Ravel, Maurice, 51
recorder, 72, 73, 80

Robison, Paula, 115

Shaffer, Elaine, 115
sonata, 25, 47, 103, 104
Syrinx, 62–63
syrinx, *see* pipes of Pan

Telemann, George Philipp, 47
transverse flute, 70, 71, 75
   see also flute, cross-blown
traverso, 73

Varese, Edgar, 108
vents, 60
vibrations, 54–55, 56
Vivaldi, Antonio, 47, 49

Wendling, Johann Baptist, 104
woodwind quartet, 24
woodwind quintet, 24